Workbook

for

It Didn't Start With You

A guide to Mark Wolynn's Book

How Inherited Family Trauma Shapes Who We Are and How to End the Cycle

Genie Reads

Table of Contents

How To Use This Workbook

Hello there!

It is with great pleasure to see that you have taken an interest in the book *"It Didn't Start with You"* by Mark Wolynn. If you have been searching for inner peace as well as that grounded sense of happiness, then perhaps you need not look any further. The troubles and trauma that plague us in our lives may not be of our own doing; and with the correct way of handling them, these previously thought to be insurmountable barriers can give way to a path filled with joy and contentment. *It Didn't Start with You* shows the structured ways of dealing with deep seated trauma and leads us through a fulfilling journey of self healing.

This workbook is meant to enhance and highlight the ideas and concepts mentioned, so that it makes it very much easier for you to take action and implement what you have learnt from the book into practical, daily usage. With the aid of this workbook, resolving traumatic issues and opening the door to holistic healing becomes much easier through the step-by-step guidance and systematic approaches highlighted within. Equipped with the knowledge and practical skillsets developed through the workbook's exercises, you will be able to overcome tough hurdles and tap into your innate potential for inner peace as well as build an aura of contented harmony around you and your loved ones. In order to absorb quicker and with a lasting impact, it is vital that you answer all the questions presented in the workbook, and answer them sincerely. Only by digging deep and giving honest answers will you be able to flash light on what truly matters to you, and get the opportunities to effect lasting positive change in your daily life.

The workbook will also feature important summaries of each individual chapter, which will be integral in helping you answer the questions contained therein. As such, for the time constrained folk, you do not necessarily need to read the main book before answering the questions in this workbook. All the crucial points have been condensed and captured for your attention. For the folks whom have already read the book, the afore mentioned salient concepts will serve well as quick reminders and gentle nudges when you are doing the questions.

Whilst attempting the questions found in the workbook, please take your time to go through it carefully. This portion is an area where speedy reading can be set aside and replaced with thoughtful ruminations. The questions will encourage you to reflect and think, sometimes very deeply, before you jump in with any answers. It will be of great benefit to you if the answers supplied are colored with the honesty of thought and tinged with sincerity. After all, no one can be as interested in your welfare as your own self.

Done in this careful, constructive way, you will be able to harness the positive change created and see it reverberate throughout many aspects of your life. For some, the honest answers may create self criticism. Take heart, know that you are not alone, and that by just the mere act of acknowledgement of mistakes made in the past, that itself is a very important step forward.

You will want to come back to these questions again after your initial foray, say after a period of 4 to 8 weeks; there really is no set in stone time length, but it is highly recommended to have at least a space of 4 weeks between the first and second attempt at the questions. This second try is really to let you see the progress you have made, both in thoughts and actions, and also to think of different angles to the same questions with your new life experiences.

You can really repeat this process as many times as you find useful. The key is always honesty in the answers and an indefatigable spirit for self development and progress.

May you be well and be happy.

Introduction

Trauma lives on. So did author Mark Wolynn conclude from his decades' worth of experience talking with people who struggled with phobias, anxiety, PTSD, obsessive thoughts, chronic illness, depression, and other similar conditions. Wolynn asserted that most of the time, the cause nor solution is not found in our experiences but rather passed on to us from older generations of our family.

This book is composed of experimental observations gathered by Wolynn when he was the director of San Francisco's Family Constellation Institute, along with recent discoveries in the science of language, epigenetics, and neuroscience. Wolynn also trained under a renowned German psychotherapist, Bert Hellinger, whose teachings on the physical and psychological effects of inherited family trauma we will discuss in the following chapters.

Wolynn shared a personal experience that led him to write the book, *It Didn't Start With You (How Inherited Family Trauma Shapes Who We Are and How to End the Cycle)*. It all began when he lost his vision. He was suffering then from ocular migraine and later found that it could soon lead to permanent blindness in both eyes. He was diagnosed with central serous retinopathy with unknown causes and no cure.

With the doctors not knowing the solution to his eyesight problem, Wolynn turned to hands-on healing, vitamins, and juice fasts. Nothing worked for him and it seemed they only made it worse. Along with his physical sight weakening, he also lost "sight" of his future and will to continue. He couldn't accept what was happening to him.

At some point, he had wondered why - why he found it extremely difficult to deal with his situation. He had known of other people, some who had it worse and yet seemed to bounce back without worries. It took him years to finally have the life-changing answer to this question.

But back then, when he had more questions than answers, he decided to leave everything behind - his family, relationship, business, and city. All he knew was he wanted to heal and with this desire, his so-called "Vision Quest" began. He went to Southeast Asia and studied with teachers whose books he read. He went to see everyone who claimed to be able to help.

He jumped from guru to guru, listening as much as he could. Yet, much to his disappointment, nothing was moving positively in his life. Until an Indonesian guru asked him, "Who are you not to have eyesight problems?" The unexpected question struck something in him. In addition, he and other listeners were earplugged and blindfolded for seventy-two hours. The purpose was to attempt to understand the craziness of their minds. Wolynn realized that his thoughts were constantly negative - always imagining the worst-case scenario of everything.

This experience somehow improved his internal vision, though his physical sight was not on the same page. He had almost healed from depression and could meditate in extensive silence. But it was in the third year of his quest that he had managed to come face-to-face with the solution. And it was a solution that he had a hard time accepting.

Wolynn was waiting in queue to meet with a spiritual master. He waited for several hours until it was his turn. Now, he expected the master to recognize his devotion. But to his surprise, the master looked through him and said, "Go home and call your parents." Oh, he did not take this easily.

After months of being alone, far from his estranged parents, Wolynn had no plans of going back home to reconnect with them. He was angry and had convinced himself that he did not need them anymore. He had his gurus, teachers, wise women, and men who could give him answers to all of life's questions. But he couldn't be any farther from the truth.

Raging mad and in denial, Wolynn ignored the spiritual master's advice and stayed on to search for another spiritual leader -- one who was known to set records straight. Just like before, he had to wait in line before his turn. When he was finally in front of the master, he heard the same line: "Go home and call your parents." By that time, he knew it was the right thing to do.

Quoting from Adam Gopnik's book *Through the Children's Gate*, "A guru gives us himself and then his system; a teacher gives us his subjects and then ourselves." Regardless of our parents' role – they could either be heroes or villains, they are still part of our lives. To push them away is to push yourself away, too. With that, Wolynn booked a one-way ticket home to Pittsburgh.

To say he was nervous is an understatement. He couldn't handle his mother's overwhelming love; he didn't even know how to deal with her touch. He used to run away from it. And when they finally saw each other after months, his mother locked him in a bone-crushing embrace. But instead of hiding, he welcomed the awkwardness and uncomfortable feeling. He understood then that he had to heal the wound from the cause.

When they finally talked and bonded, Wolynn heard stories from his mother that ultimately linked to his present experiences. For one, his mother got severely sick when he was two and had to be hospitalized. When his mother came back, he wasn't the same. He no longer trusted her and pushed her away every chance he could. With her being gone for a while, he assumed she was inconsistent. From there, it only worsened.

His mother also experienced a difficult childbirth with him, which resulted in a forceps delivery. She was honest that she had trouble holding him at that time due to his partially collapsed skull and heavy bruising. In the same way, he would get traumatic memories about this experience whenever he presented new projects – akin to his newly born babies - in public.

Wolynn's parents separated when he was thirteen. As he worked on his relationship with his mother, he also reached out to his father - a construction worker and retired marine sergeant. Communication between father and son was never good if it ever existed. But, this time and in person, he spoke up and admitted that he missed his father. With that, they tried to keep talking to resolve whatever needed resolving between them.

"You're a good father," Wolynn said. Just like with his mother, he kept the fire burning with him. And one day, as they were having lunch together, which had become routine, his father 'fessed up and said that he never thought his son had loved him. At that moment, their hearts opened for each other. The vulnerability of the situation prompted them both to express and accept each others' love.

Wolynn realized that the strain in his relationship with his parents was more of his problem than theirs. They have always loved him but not how he expected them to. This experience led him to develop his language of fear. He felt helpless, ruined, and alone. It wasn't until he repaired what was broken that he accepted the love his parents always had for him.

Wolynn understood the significance of the wonderful teachers and masters who taught and guided him throughout the months of being lost and resentful. But if he was being honest with himself, it was his problematic eyesight that brought him halfway through the world and then back to his parents.

Without noticing it, he no longer minded what was happening with his eyes. His visual journey became a self-healing story. And then, when he was least worried about it, his sight came back - with a stellar 20/20 vision. So ultimately, healing isn't found outside ourselves; it lies from within. We only need to be willing to dig a little deeper.

Language is an essential factor in healing. While most theorists believe that it weakens with trauma, Wolynn disagrees. As a poet, words have always been his best tool of expression and eventually, of healing. It was vital for him to understand the words helpless, ruined, and alone. Discovering what they meant to set him on the right track.

Wolynn maximized his knowledge in this factor as a workshop leader and teacher to develop the core language approach. It's important to use the right words in unraveling trauma in all its ugliness. Sometimes, we discover that the language we've been trying hard to find only lies within ourselves or is borrowed from our family.

In this book, you will learn more stories that are much similar to Wolynn's. There will be excerpts from training, individual sessions, and workshops. Together, we will learn how powerful language is in discovering the causes of inherited trauma and ending the cycle altogether. Buckle up and get ready to start your journey to healing.

Part 1: The Web of Family Trauma

Ch 1: Traumas Lost and Found

Summary

Have you ever watched a movie where a character gets into a car accident and then wakes up later on at the hospital? Upon gaining consciousness, the first line they will say is: "What happened to me?" The same thing happens to us when we have traumatic experiences. We become disoriented and our thoughts go crazy.

Instead of clear, coherent thoughts, we have dispersed images, body sensations, and fragments of memory trapped in our unconscious mind. When we experience an event that is remotely similar to the past, it triggers the original trauma. This leads to the person reliving the same thing over and over again. This tendency is called *traumatic reenactment*, or as Sigmund Freud called it, *repetition compulsion* where the mind unconsciously relives what was unresolved in an attempt to resolve it. Freud's supporter Carl Jung postulated that something unresolved does not go away, it only reappears through fortune or fate.

Recent studies by Dutch psychiatrist Bessel van der Kolk show that the speech center shuts down during a traumatic experience. It's the same thing as when you'd say "I'm at a loss for words." Traumatized, our brain is incapable of thinking well, making it hard for us to say anything. But the truth is that this just gets rerouted to form a secret language of fear.

In addition to what has been discussed, it was also discovered that one must explore up to three generations of family history to unravel the patterns of suffering and trauma. Different kinds of tragedies can cause distress levels that carry on to the next generation. It turns out that an individual's trauma is much more than that.

Wolynn shared a story of Jesse, who was once a straight-A student and star athlete. He shared that the night after his nineteenth birthday, he woke up at around 3:30 AM and was not able to go back to sleep again. Jesse told Wolynn that he felt freezing and had this irrational fear that if he went back to sleep, he wouldn't wake up again.

Insomnia became a serious problem for Jesse, which led to his downfall: losing the sports scholarship he worked so hard to earn and then dropping out of college. When they met, Jesse showed signs of having become someone who had lost all hope. For one, he spoke in a monotone. But not having enough sleep for years despite having visited a sleep clinic and consulted with a naturopathic physician, two psychologists, and three doctors, losing hope was bound to happen.

Wolynn probed deeper into Jesse's condition and asked if someone in his family had traumas linked to being nineteen and in the cold. As it turned out, his Uncle Colin died of hypothermia when he was also nineteen. The death was too traumatic and brutal that Jesse wasn't told about this until then. He was unconsciously displaying the same condition that led to Colin's death. His fear of falling asleep was Colin's fear of letting go and dying out in the cold.

Once the connection was made, Jesse understood why it was happening to him. He realized that he had created a strong bond with his family's past and present. He could finally start healing. It was cases like Jesse's that allowed scientists to determine biological markers – proof that trauma is passed down to the next generation.

One of the world's leading researchers of PTSD, Rachel Yehuda is a professor of neuroscience and psychiatry at Mt. Sinai School of Medicine in New York. In her observations on Holocaust survivors and their children, she discovered that they had relatively low cortisol. The same goes for war veterans, mothers who developed PTSD after the WTC attacks, and their children.

When a person suffers from chronic PTSD, their cortisol production becomes suppressed, which they can pass on to their children. Some of the stress-related disorders such as chronic fatigue syndrome, chronic pain syndrome, and PTSD are all caused by low levels of cortisol. Further, 50 to 70 percent of PTSD patients meet the criteria for anxiety or mood disorder, even major depression.

What does this prove? It simply shows that people are most likely to suffer from PTSD symptoms if one of their parents has PTSD. This could lead to anxiety or depression. This was what happened with Gretchen, a 39-year-old woman who wanted to end her life before reaching her 40th birthday.

After years of therapy, group sessions, and antidepressants, Gretchen flat-out told Wolynn that she was going to jump into a vat of molten steel at her brother's workplace. She said her body will be incinerated or vaporized before she reaches the bottom. The words she used hit a nerve with Wolynn because he'd heard them before. Those were the words commonly spoken by other patients who had experienced the holocaust and families of victims of the tragedy.

Wolynn asked Gretchen if she had relatives who were Jewish or had experienced the Holocaust. Gretchen then remembered her grandmother who was born into a Jewish family back in Poland. Although she converted to Catholicism in 1946 when she moved to the United States with her husband, her grandmother's family was brought to Auschwitz where they were gassed and incinerated.

Just like in Jesse's family, nobody spoke about this incident within Gretchen's family because of its brutality. Wolynn explained the connection and something clicked within Gretchen. It was the first time she understood the reason behind her depression and suicidal thoughts. To take this realization further, Wolynn instructed her to imagine standing in her grandmother's shoes. Gretchen then described overwhelming feelings of guilt, loss, aloneness, grief, and isolation.

Gretchen and Jesse were both able to process their trauma once they realized and understood where it was coming from. This was where healing became available to them. Sometimes, awareness requires the presence of an innate experience. Both individuals had remnants of trauma within them even if they never had any personal connection with the terrible events.

Jesse started to relive the trauma Colin experienced minutes before he died through his insomnia when he turned nineteen. Meanwhile, Gretchen has carried his grandmother's suicidal thoughts and guilt through her depression for as long as she could remember. A pain this great is often tossed to the side, which is why it is passed on to the next generation - it wasn't resolved immediately.

Lessons

1. Traumatic reenactment or repetition compulsion is the state where the mind relives an unresolved trauma in an attempt to deal with it.

2. Problems such as depression, insomnia, and other illnesses that occur to us out of the blue may come from familial traumas.

3. A trauma that has not been resolved in one generation may be passed on to the next generation.

4. Healing is only possible when the present generation acknowledges that the trauma was not theirs to carry in the first place.

Issues Surrounding the Subject Matter

1. Why is it important to know the source of your trauma?

2. Why do we suffer from problems that we did not cause?

3. Are you ready to dig deeper and finally start the journey to self-healing?

Goals

1. How is your present trauma related to the traumas of your family's previous generations?

2. How are you going to heal your pains?

3. How are you going to face the cause of the trauma?

Action Steps

1. Think back to issues or problems that you've been having lately. Anything. Keep your focus on that as you move forward with this workbook.

2. Revisit how your concern or problem started. Did it begin when you were still a child? What age were you? What happened before that?

3. Revisit conversations you had with your folks, anything that could be similar to the problem you have now.

Checklist

1. Try to know more about your history. Was your family affected by the Holocaust or another terrible moment in history? Do you come from a direct line of soldiers deployed to fight in wars?

2. Keep an open mind for the following chapters. This could go beyond medicines and therapies.

3. Try to find someone (in your family) that you can run to for questions regarding your family, you may have many to ask them in the following chapters.

Ch 2: Three Generations of Shared Family History: The Family Body

Summary

Before you were born, the egg you were conceived with was already present in your mother's body. Note that a female's eggs develop during the fifth month as an unborn infant. This means that when your grandmother was five months pregnant with your mother, a part of you was already present - three generations in one body, biologically sharing the same environment.

On the other side, the parent sperm that fertilized your mother's egg was already present while he was still in his mother's womb. While some people may be amazed by how science works, this is not considered a recent discovery. Textbooks on embryology have already discussed the phenomenon in depth. But with this knowledge on top of the Yehuda studies, we can now trace how biological remnants are carried forward.

Cellular biology plays a big role in this. It was originally believed that genes alone make up the blueprint of an individual. Guided accordingly, a person will grow up the way they are expected to. Bruce Lipton, a pioneering cell biologist, indicates that human DNA can be affected by positive and negative emotions, thoughts, and beliefs. Everything a mother experiences and feels can alter the genetic print of the unborn child.

A great deal of research has been undertaken, demonstrating how a pregnant woman's stress can affect her unborn child, even as early as the first trimester. This is why Lipton highlights the significance of *conscious parenting*. This entails that the parents should be aware that if they allow carrying a child in a stressful environment, the stress will be passed on to the offspring.

It would help us a good deal to understand the scientific field of epigenetics in order to appreciate the value of *conscious parenting*. Epigenetics is the study of heritable variations in gene activity that don't involve alterations in DNA sequence. Back then, it was a common belief that the chromosomal DNA we receive from our parents plays the biggest role in whom we become. But in contrast to that theory, the physical attributes only take up less than 2 percent of our total DNA, while the rest is made up of cDNA or noncoding DNA.

Noncoding DNA depends on external factors such as environmental stressors and stressful emotions. It allows the unborn infant to adapt to its outside world even before being born. On the upside, cDNA helps an individual easily adjust to the real world. But on the downside, it can make the individual too sensitive and overly affected even when danger is not present. And when someone is constantly stressed for no reason, it could lead to disorders and diseases.

Epigenetic tags, which link to DNA and instruct cells to either activate or suppress a particular gene, are responsible for these adaptive modifications in cells. While the DNA's sequence itself is unaffected by these epigenetic markers, its expression is. Epigenetic tagging, according to research, may be responsible for variations in how we handle stress as we age.

DNA methylation, which prevents proteins from adhering to a gene and suppresses its expression, is the most prevalent epigenetic tag. DNA methylation can lock "useful" or "unhelpful" genes in the "off" position, which can have a favorable or negative impact on human health. Researchers have discovered anomalies in DNA methylation that can be passed down to the next generations along with a propensity for problems with physical or mental health when stressors or trauma occur.

The tiny noncoding RNA molecule known as microRNA is another epigenetic factor that has a substantial impact on the control of gene expression. Stress-related variations in microRNA levels, like DNA methylation, can have an impact on the way genes are expressed throughout successive generations. The genes for CRF1 (corticotropin-releasing hormone receptor) and CRF2 are among the many genes impacted by stress. People with anxiety and depression have been found to have higher amounts of these genes. It is possible to inherit the CRF1 and CRF2 genes from stressed moms who have comparable stress levels.

Yehuda and her team at the Mount Sinai Hospital in New York revealed that gene alterations could be passed down from parents to their offspring in a study that was published in Biological Psychiatry in August 2015. They discovered that Holocaust-affected Jews and their offspring had an identical genetic pattern after analyzing a specific area of a gene linked to stress control. Epigenetic marks specifically on the same area of the gene on both the parent and the child. When they compared the findings with those from Jewish families who did not reside in Europe during the war, they concluded that parental trauma was the only cause of the children's gene modifications.

Numerous recent studies have shown that parental traumatic events might affect the gene expression and stress levels of their offspring. Native American kids are among the most recent victims of transgenerational trauma in the modern world, along with the children of Holocaust survivors, World Trade Center assault survivors, and survivors of the Cambodian genocide.

It's concerning that the list keeps growing. As survivors unwittingly pass their experiences on to succeeding generations, violence, conflict, and oppression continue to plant the seeds of generational reliving. Yehuda asserts that children of PTSD-afflicted moms are threefold more likely than kids in her control groups to receive a PTSD diagnosis. She also discovered that when either parent had PTSD, the likelihood of the child developing depression, anxiety, or substance misuse increased by three to four times.

Grandparents who have PTSD can pass it on to younger generations. Gretchen mentioned in the earlier chapter is a prime example of how war-related trauma can perpetuate itself and impact the victim's grandchildren. Traumas can cause us to relive trauma symptoms from the past, including those related to war as well as traumas related to any incident severe enough to upset the emotional balance in our family, such as an early death, a crime, a suicide, or a sudden and unexpected loss.

Scientists have just lately begun to comprehend the biochemical processes that take place when trauma is passed on. Researchers have used animal studies to learn more. These investigations give us a window through which to study the impacts of hereditary stress in our lives due to the strong genetic similarity between people and mice. Animal research also requires less time than human research because data from multigenerational experiments can be obtained in just twelve weeks compared to researching people, which could take more than 60 years.

In one experiment, female mice were prevented from caring for their young for up to three hours a day for the first two weeks of their lives. Later on, in life, their grown offspring exhibited traits that people associate with depression. As the mice aged, the symptoms appeared to get worse. Remarkably, some of the male species did not exhibit the behaviors but instead seemed to pass on the behavioral alterations to the female progeny through epigenetic means.

Another rat study found that adult rats who received low amounts of mother care were more sensitive to stress and anxiety than adult rats who received elevated amounts of maternal care. Multiple generations of this stress pattern have been recorded. It is well known that babies who have been taken from their mothers often struggle as a result. In experiments with male mice, newborns that were taken away from their moms showed lifelong increases in their susceptibility to stress and produced offspring that displayed the same stress patterns over multiple generations.

The intriguing aspect of mouse research is that it has allowed science to demonstrate how problems faced by one generation can indeed be passed on to the following. The results from human experiments spanning numerous generations are still pending because a human generation lasts roughly twenty years. But given that the study's findings showed stress can be passed down by at least three generations of mice, the experts hypothesized that children born to human parents who had a traumatic or stressful experience would also probably do the same, not just to their children but to their grandchildren as well.

Lessons

1. We are carrying three generations of trauma based on cellular biology and epigenetics.

2. We cannot change our DNAs but we can control how we make them react.

3. Multiple studies prove that it is possible to inherit PTSD and manifest it through different illnesses such as depression, anxiety, substance misuse, and more.

Issues Surrounding the Subject Matter

1. Is there something that happened to your grandparents that might have been the cause of your trauma now?

2. How is your relationship with your grandparents?

3. Why do you think you were the one who inherited the trauma?

Goals

1. How are you going to find out the things that happened in the past, especially something that involved your grandparents and parents?

2. How will you know which stories are related to you?

3. How will you know that a certain event affected your adulthood?

Action Steps

1. List down a summary of the tragic events that you know happened in the past starting from the childhood of your **grandparents** up to their adulthood. It can be related to your worries or not.

2. List down a summary of the tragic events that you know happened in the past starting from the childhood of your **parents** up to their adulthood. It can be related to your worries or not.

3. Relate these events to what happened to you. Observe if any rings a bell.

Checklist

1. Read more on epigenetics and cellular biology to have a clearer grasp of how these two subjects play their role in generational trauma.

2. Check the research results of mice related to trauma to get a quick idea of how it works with humans.

3. Look at images of your grandparents and parents as kids, if possible. Most of the time, memorabilia like this help you relate to them.

Ch 3: The Family Mind

Summary

Through our mother, we inherit some of our grandmother's maternal qualities. The challenges our grandmother faced as a child or while raising our mother, the painful memories of people she loved who passed away too soon—these things filtered to some extent into the mothering our mother received from our grandmother. The same would probably apply to our grandmother's mothering if we backtracked to the generation before hers.

Besides inheriting our parents' traits, their parenting style impacts how we interact with others, how we view ourselves, and how we raise our children. Parents often emulate the parenting they got, for better or worse. These patterns emerge before we are even born and seem to be programmed into the brain. Our neurological circuitry largely develops as a result of our mother's interactions with us while we are still in the womb.

The delicate relationship that is formed between a mother and her newborn can be affected and is more likely to be broken when the woman bears inherited trauma or has suffered a disruption in the attachment with her mother. Winifred Gallagher, a behavior science writer, says that when an infant is away from its mother, it suffers from psychological and physical withdrawal. A neonatologist, Dr. Raylene Phillips adds that if separation is extended, the baby will give up.

Mark Wolynn shared his experience as he also knew the feeling of wanting to give up. His grandmother Ida faced a traumatic experience when she was still a baby. Her mother Sora died when Ida was only two years old. Sora's parents blamed Ida's father, Andrew, whom they described as a gambling addict, for the death of their daughter. The story that Ida heard was that Andrew spent all their money on gambling and Sora spent many nights begging him to come home, got sick with pneumonia, and died.

After Sora's death, Andrew was dismissed from the family, and Ida was brought up by her grandparents. Without a doubt, Ida had a pretty happy childhood with her loving grandparents. She'd smile when she recalls memories with them. However, Ida also felt all the pain and heartaches her mother suffered when she was still in Sora's womb. Sora's death shattered Ida emotionally.

Not only was Wolynn's mother fostered by an orphan who was unable to provide her with the maternal care she needed, but she also carried the visceral anguish of Ida's early mother-child separation. Ida was physically there in his mother's life, but she was incapable of articulating the depth of feeling that would have helped his mother grow. The emotional link that was lost was also passed down to his mother.

On the other side, Wolynn's grandfather Harry also had a troubling childhood having had his mother die during childbirth when he was still a five-year-old kid. Samuel, Harry's father blamed himself for causing the pregnancy in the first place. He also remarried a woman who did not care about Harry. Wolynn's mother often narrates how Harry used to starve and would eat junk from garbage cans to survive.

Three generations of trauma are visible in Wolynn's family tree. It was up to Mark himself to rebuild his relationship with his mother. Events that evoke feelings of abandonment or rejection may be enough to cause the consequences to resurface in our unconscious and manifest as somatic memories in our bodies. Because the trauma started so early, it frequently goes unnoticed and remains concealed. Bonding damage can be passed on through the generations if the pattern is not deliberately altered.

Bert Hellinger, the well-known German psychologist, has written several works on the idea that we acquire and "relive" elements of familial trauma. He learned from his rich history that these impressions eventually become the family pattern as family members unintentionally relive the pain of the past. However, the traumatic incident that is repeated is not necessarily an identical reproduction of the first one.

As an example, Wolynn shared how an individual named John came to see him after being released from prison. John claimed that he was innocent but due to the evidence held against him, he was forced to take a plea deal. It turns out that John's father was accused of murder way back in the 60s. Everyone in their family knew that his father was guilty but when he was acquitted due to a technicality, no one spoke about it again. In a way, justice was served.

In Hellinger's opinion, unconscious loyalty is the process that leads to descendants repeating errors or misdeeds of those that had come before them and is responsible for a great deal of family sorrow. People sometimes think that the cause of their difficulty is their own experience because they are unable to recognize the root of their symptoms as coming from a previous generation, which leaves them unable to find a solution.

No one may be excluded from a family system for any reason at all; every person has the same opportunity to be a part of one. When Hellinger said *everyone*, he meant your grandparents' and parents' earlier partners, a criminal uncle, a mother's half-brother, an aborted baby, a stillborn sister, etc. By dying, leaving, or having already departed, they leave a gap in the system which then allows our father, mother, grandma, or grandpa to enter this gap and ultimately, give birth to us.

According to Hellinger, a person who is rejected or excluded from the family system may subsequently be represented by another person in the system. By acting in a similar manner or by experiencing part of the excluded person's misery again, the latter person may share or replicate the destiny of the earlier individual. So, the pain of the family is passed on to the next generations.

The German psychologist also added that each member should carry on their fate despite its severity. No one can try to assume a family member's fate without experiencing some sort of anguish. This form of pain is referred to by Hellinger as "entanglement." When you are entangled, you unwittingly take on the emotions, signs, traits, or struggles of a former member of your family system and carry them as if they were your own. A family's later offspring may frequently bear the grandparents' unsolved traumas.

When the mother-child tie between siblings is broken, each kid may show the effects of their separation from the mother on them in a different way. One youngster may develop into a people-pleaser, another may become argumentative, while yet another may grow socially isolated and have very little contact with others. But then, other kids and their siblings don't appear to have experienced any kind of family stress, probably because a strong link was formed either between them and their father or mother.

There are no hard and fast guidelines dictating how each child is affected when it comes to siblings and family trauma that is passed down to them. The decisions siblings make and the experiences they follow can be influenced by a variety of factors, in addition to their birth order and gender. Wolynn discovered that the majority of us retain some traces of our ancestors. However, many other unmeasurable factors also come into play that can have an impact on how deeply ingrained family traumas can be – self-awareness, the capacity for self-soothing, and the ability to experience a potent internal healing experience.

Psychiatrist Dr. Norman Doidge, the author of *The Brain That Changes Itself*, says that psychotherapy is converting our ghosts into ancestors. Allowing oneself to be affected by an event or picture powerful enough to eclipse the internalized emotions and sensations associated with past traumas is one helpful exercise we can do for ourselves.

Carl Jung first used the phrase "active imagination" in 1913 to describe a method that involves using imagery, sometimes from dreams, to communicate with the subconscious and reveal hidden information. With guided imagery techniques widely available to decrease stress, reduce anxiety, improve athletic performance, and aid with specific anxieties and phobias, the concept of visualization for recovery has recently acquired considerable momentum.

Making the connection between our concerns and symptoms and what is behind them already creates fresh avenues for resolution. When we learn something new, it can sometimes be enough to change the terrible memories we still have in our bodies and start a primal release that we can physically feel. We start to develop an internal sense of well-being that begins to fight with our old trauma responses and their capacity to mislead us as new feelings, ideas, sensations, and a new mind map get imprinted.

Dr. Dawson Church, author of the best-seller *The Genie in Your Genes*, narrates how meditation, visualization, and concentrating on positive prayers, thoughts, and emotions can impact gene activation and positively change our health. A study that was published in the book *Psychoneuroendocrinology* in 2013 showed that meditators exhibited clear genetic and molecular changes after just eight hours of meditation, including reduced levels of pro-inflammatory genes, which could help speed up their physical recovery from stressful situations.

To this, Rachel Yehuda added that we can't change our DNA. Even if we changed how it functions, it would still be the same. We will learn that it's quite improbable for anyone to live life fully trauma-free. Traumas do not go away when a person passes away; instead, they search for a fruitful site for healing in the future generations' offspring. Fortunately, people are resilient and can recover from the majority of traumas. This is a possibility at any point in our lives. What we need to recover is to gain the correct knowledge and equipment for it.

Lessons

1. Our parents have inherited our grandparents' parenting style, which will also reflect in our adult life.

2. A child's pattern for controlling emotions, ideas, and behaviors is formed through these early interactions.

3. If there is someone in the family who was once rejected or ignored, they may be represented in the future generation.

4. Guided imagery techniques are known to be effective in reducing stress and anxiety.

Issues Surrounding the Subject Matter

1. Did someone in your family do something illegal or morally wrong, but was not punished for it?

2. Is there a member of your family who is not talked about or completely forgotten? Why? What happened?

3. Were you able to manage your emotions as a kid? Why or why not?

Goals

1. How would you know about the rejected family members you haven't heard from or met?

2. How does your problem align with the rejected or forgotten family member?

3. How will you create guided imagery techniques?

4. How does your parents' parenting style affect your present?.

Action Steps

1. Ask the difficult questions. There might be hidden family members whom your parents do not want to talk about.

2. Revisit your childhood and think back on how your parents raised you, as much as you can. Compare them to the parenting styles you are aware of now (as an adult).

3. Create imagery techniques such as visualization and forced dreaming to lessen your worries.

Checklist

1. Talk to your friends or other trusted individuals that already have kids. Compare their parenting style to the parenting style you received as a child.

2. Search for visualization samples that you can use in decreasing your stress and trauma levels.

3. Search for big news that happened in your hometown during the time you were a child, or just recently born. It may bring some light to perhaps some of your trauma.

Ch 4: The Core Language Approach

Summary

When fragments of old trauma recur inside of us, these pieces leave traces. We frequently find ourselves connected to unsettled traumas, some of which don't even belong to us, by clues in the shape of emotionally charged phrases and sentences that convey our darkest anxieties. Wolynn refers to these traumas as core language, which may be communicated without words. Impulses, emotions, physical sensations, behaviors, and even disease symptoms might be among them.

The tale of Hansel and Gretel is well known to everybody. Hansel lays a path of breadcrumbs in the forest to secure their safe journey home since he fears they won't be able to find their way back. We perform the identical action, but rather than leaving breadcrumbs, we instead leave a verbal trail that might help us reorient ourselves. Just like the fictional duo, we could stray too deeply into the jungle of our anxieties to even recognize where we are. We can end up turning to medication rather than following the correct path.

It may be possible to explain what happens to our speech when we're overwhelmed by emotions by knowing how stressful memories are preserved. Declarative memory, also known as explicit or narrative memory, is the capacity to consciously recall information or experiences, and it is one of the two primary categories into which long-term memory is frequently subdivided. It depends on language to store, categorize, and organize experiences and information that will later turn into retrievable memories.

The other type is non-declarative memory, known as implicit, sensorimotor, or procedural memory, which works without conscious remembering. Without having to repeat the procedures, it enables us to automatically recall what we've previously learnt. These memories, like our traumatic experiences, are not always simple to put into words. We cannot adequately capture or "declare" a memory in the form of a narrative when it is so overpowering that we are unable to speak. Storytelling demands language.

We can no longer fully access our memories of the incident without the use of language. They enter our unconsciousness after being lost and undeclared. Our enormous unconscious seems to include both our unresolved traumatic memories and our ancestors' unresolved traumatic experiences. We appear to relive portions of an ancestor's memories and claim them as our own in this collective unconscious.

The prior experiments on mice offer some indication of how traumas are passed across the generations, but the precise mechanism by which this transfer occurs in people is still not entirely known. And yet, even if we're not entirely sure how an ancestor's unfinished business becomes ingrained in us, it seems to provide solace when this connection is made.

Mark Wolynn shows the different tools that will help in linking the connection between unexplainable emotions and past events. Each one has a set of inquiries that aims to bring out an inner experience or feeling that has never been brought to light before. Once there is enough data, the *core language map* will start to show. The words used will decide the path which we will undertake.

There probably was a core language map in place before we were ever born. We may have been keeping it for our father or grandma. We are now given the chance to determine how we acquired it and where it came from. Our core language map can help us find family members who linger like ghosts, unnoticed and uncared for. Our past is only waiting to be found. Everything we need to complete the voyage, including the language, the words, and the map, is right now inside of us.

In the third chapter, Wolynn shared how visualization tools can make new neural pathways in our brains. You'll discover activities designed to help you break free from the limitations of habitual thinking in the subsequent chapters. They are intended to stir things up so that the underlying unconscious streams might come to the surface. Each activity builds upon the previous one. There's no need to stress over giving the proper or wrong response. Let your natural curiosity lead you to self-healing.

Lessons

1. The core language is composed of words, impulses, emotions, etc. that manifest in the form of trauma.

2. When we cannot properly address a trauma, it gets lost in our minds as a scattered memory.

3. The core language map is formed to connect all the sections in identifying the source of trauma.

Issues Surrounding the Subject Matter

1. What is a trauma for you?

2. What words do you use to describe the trauma you are experiencing? Why do you use these words?

3. What actions do you take or impulses do you feel are related to the issue you have?

Goals

1. How do you interpret your trauma?

2. How will you create your core language map?

3. How do we access our unconsciousness?

Action Steps

1. Break down your trauma. As explained, trauma comes in verbal and nonverbal cues. Try to point out what words you use to describe your fear and what actions you do concerning it.

2. Observe if you repeat similar actions that your mother and father did before.

3. Try to convert your actions to words. Observe what words you'd use to describe them.

Checklist

1. Learn about the different non-verbal cues that you can look for in yourself. Know what they mean.

2. Understand the difference between declarative and non-declarative memories.

3. Get your mind (and heart) ready for the following chapters, as they will open up thoughts and memories of the past.

Ch 5: The Four Unconscious Themes

Summary

One thing is certain: life always sends us ahead with some unresolved issue from the past, whether it is from the womb when we inherit our parents' emotions, from our early relationships with our mothers, or through implicit loyalty or familial tragedies.

We fool ourselves when we imagine we can control how our lives unfold. Our intentions and deeds don't always match up. We could want to be healthy, yet overindulge in unhealthy food or find reasons to avoid workouts. The worst bit is that the precise thing blocking us from moving forward is sometimes invisible to us, which keeps us upset and perplexed.

Often, we blame the inadequacies in our upbringing, the unfortunate events in our childhood, or our parents' shortcomings. We repeatedly return to the same ideas. However, remembering in this manner rarely improves the situation. Our criticisms just serve to reinforce our ongoing displeasure since we are unable to identify the cause of the problem. So now, we will unravel four themes that hinder our progress. But first, we revisit the beginning of it all.

The path was uncomplicated. Our parents brought us here and shared a spark with us. Although we are not the originator of that current, we are connected to it through our parents. The spark and our family history have just been transmitted to us. It is also possible to become aware of its internal existence. This spark is what gives us life. It may be pulsating inside of you right now.

After birth, that vital energy continues to exist. Even if you don't feel connected to your parents, it still flows from them to you. We feel more receptive to life's opportunities when our relationship with our parents is open and flowing. The life energy that is accessible to us may seem constrained if our relationship with our parents is somehow harmed. But we have the tools to cure ourselves. We begin by evaluating the relationship we have with our parents.

Our parents give forth a natural life energy that freely flows to us. All we have to do is accept it. Think of the life force as the primary electrical cable entering your house – the additional cables that diverge into the different rooms according to the power's primary cable. No matter how well we wire our home, the flow will be affected if our link to the main line is weakened.

Here are the four unconscious themes that disrupt the flow of life:

1.   We have connected with a parent.
2.   We have pushed away a parent.

3.   We have suffered from a break in our early relationship with our mother.
4.   We have identified with a member of our family system that is not our parents.

Any of these themes have the potential to prevent us from thriving and succeeding in our objectives. They may restrict our prosperity, health, and energy. The themes are relational in the sense that they discuss various facets of our relationships with our parents and other members of our family unit. Understanding the themes and knowing where to search for them can help us recognize which ones are active within us and prevent us from living life to the fullest.

Three out of the four unconscious themes involve suffering a disconnection from our parents. While there are other factors to consider, most of these are no longer unconscious. This includes personal traumas we encounter in which we are aware of their existence but still feel inadequate to resolve them. Another factor is guilt, which as we heard from John in the previous chapter, also passes on to our descendants.

The next step is to dig deeper into the interruptions that are linked directly to our parents or other members of the family system, or both. First, we need to identify whether we have merged with our parents' struggles psychologically, emotionally, or physically. Do you recognize the pain of your parents within you?

Many of us unwittingly adopt our parents' suffering. Maybe when we were little we thought we could make them happy by sharing or mending things. They wouldn't have to bear it alone if we carried it as well. However, this is fantasy thinking, which simply increases dissatisfaction. The children reflect on the issues in the parents' relationships. When we merge with a parent, we unknowingly share a part of their life experience—often a bad one. Many times, we repeat or replay events without making the connection that may enlighten us.

This was visible in Gavin's story. He was thirty-four when he lost his family's savings in an attempt to stay afloat when he was fired from his job. The event pushed him into a downward path to depression. During his session with Wolynn, they made the connection that years back, his father went through the same thing. Gavin's father also lost their family's savings which resulted in him losing Gavin and the rest of the family.

After a decade of not speaking with his father, Gavin found it surreal to have such a strong connection to his father's trauma. But this realization is what he needed to get back on his feet. He worked to repair his relationship with him through a series of awkward phone calls until eventually, they did meet in person. Slowly, Gavin's depression lifted.

We prolong the family's pain and stop the life energy that is accessible to us and the generations that precede us by seeking to carry or share our parent's load. It is crucial to maintain and preserve the essence of the parent-child connection even when we are providing for sick or old parents who are unable to care for themselves, rather than demeaning their dignity.

It is also important that we acknowledge if we have ever pushed away our parents by cutting them off, blaming, rejecting, or judging them negatively. We must mend our strained bonds with our parents if we aim to genuinely enjoy life and feel joy. Our parents are the key to the hidden talents, creative powers, and difficulties that are also a part of our ancestry, in addition to giving us life and making us who we are. Our parents—and the traumas they've gone through or passed down to us—hold the key to our recovery, whether they're still alive or not, whether we're close to them or not.

Broken relationships can result from traumatic experiences in our family's past and can continue for generations until we put a stop to them by taking a constructive approach to the issue. We can only overcome the grief that keeps us from fully embracing our life by doing this. Finding a space inside ourselves where we can mellow and not bristle when we think about our parents is crucial, even if at first we can only make the shift on an internal level.

This strategy could be in opposition to what you've learned. A large portion of traditional talk therapy places the parents at the center of the problem. Our old tales can hold us captive, but if we learn the deeper stories that lie underneath them, they can liberate us. That freedom's wellspring is already within us, just waiting to be discovered. We are inclined to carry over the feelings, characteristics, and actions we find repulsive in our parents. It's our unintentional method of showing them love and of reintegrating them into our lives. In Gavin's life, we observed how that pattern subtly manifested itself.

Our bodies might experience discomfort, stiffness, or numbness as a result of being rejected by our parents. Until our abandoned parent is lovingly felt inside of us, our bodies will experience some degree of restlessness. Often, repairing our connection with our parents starts on the inside. Sometimes we have to make a step into our inner world before we can take a stride into the outside world.

A strong connection with our parents has been demonstrated to be associated with excellent health in addition to increasing the level of support and comfort we experience in life. Particularly concerning our early connections, those with our mothers might act as a model for future partnerships. This is what happened with Tricia as she went on with her life with short-lived romantic relationships.

Often, she'd describe her partners as "distant, cold, insensitive." Unknowingly, these are also the words she would use in describing her mother. Her rejection of her mother is the cause of all the failed relationships. Going back to her mother's history, it turns out that Tricia's grandmother was also dubbed as selfish and emotionally unavailable.

Her grandmother was sent on to live with her uncle and aunt, which is why she grew up resenting everything. This anger resonated during her daughter's or Tricia's mother's upbringing. Unknowingly, it was also passed down to Tricia's upbringing. But as she understood the root, Tricia felt compassion toward her mother.

Experiencing a pause in the early relationship with our mother also plays a big role in our adult lives. Like your mother's and grandmother's experiences, a break in the mother-child tie in earlier generations might have an impact on your relationship with your mother. Later generations may still be affected by these early experiences. You might never know the answers to these questions if you're estranged from your folks or if they're dead, particularly if you were a very small child at the time of the break.

The initial years of our lives are not well-remembered by the brain. It takes a little while beyond the age of two for the connections between the hippocampus and the prefrontal cortex to properly mature. The hippocampus is the area of the brain responsible for creating, organizing, and storing memories. As a result, the pain of an early separation would be remembered in bits and pieces as images, feelings, and bodily sensations. The feelings and experiences might be hard to comprehend without the tale.

Sometimes the relationship is severed without a physical rupture. She might be there physically, but she might be inconsistent or emotionally aloof. For a child's psychological and emotional well-being throughout the first few years of life, a mother's presence and consistency are crucial. If our relationship with our mother was severed at a young age, we may need to put together some hints from both our own and our mother's past.

It's another thing if we have unconsciously connected with a member of our family system that is not our parents. Even when we have a close, loving relationship with our parents, we occasionally find ourselves unable to articulate the challenging emotions we experience. We frequently believe that the issue comes from within us and can be resolved if we look hard enough. We might revisit worries and sensations that aren't ours and believe they are ours until we find the true critical incident in our family's past.

Here comes the story of ten-year-old Todd and how he assaulted his neighbor with a stick, which resulted in a wound that needed forty stitches to close up. Despite treatment, Todd still displayed violent actions. Here's when his father, Earl, narrated his father's story to Wolynn. It turns out that Todd's grandfather was a violent man and had stabbed someone in a club brawl. The grandfather was never brought to prison and was able to live his life fully.

It turned out that the grandfather's father and grandfather were also involved in some kind of murder while earlier generations of the family were killed in a gang-related incident. Earl realized that his late father was merely a victim of generational trauma. For the first time in his life, he felt compassion toward his father. He also told this to his son, Todd, who unknowingly was reliving the traumas from generations before.

To have a deeper grasp of how the four unconscious themes get set in motion, let us use this example. First, something tragic happens. The eldest brother dies suddenly, leaving behind a two-year-old younger brother and grieving parents. Here is how the devastating event may affect the surviving child:

1.　The child could reject one of the parents.

Either parent might lose the will to live because of the intensifying grief. Either could start drinking or gambling, or any other activity that distracts them from being home. There's also a possibility that the parents blame each other for what happened. The surviving son would feel the parents' negative emotions.

As a response, the child could shield himself from the emotions that he does not understand. Once he grows up, he might blame his parents for the distance and lack of attention given to him without understanding how they felt about the death of his older brother.

2.　The child might experience an interrupted bond with his mother.

As expected, the death of a child would ruin his mother's heart. For a long time, the mother might withdraw from everything and get stuck with her grief. The tragedy will become the interruption that gets in between them.

He would only sense that she was bonding with him one minute and then, she was suddenly gone the next. His body would release chemicals that would make him aware of the inconsistency, keeping him on watch. He could then lose faith in her because of her seeming inconsistencies and concern that she might "vanish" on him at any moment.

3. The child might merge with either parent's pain.

The younger kid may feel the weight of his parents' suffering as if it were his own when the elder child has passed away. The ripple effects of bereavement may cause the entire family to become stiff. He would try to bear his mother's depression or his father's anguish as if he had some magical ability to take it away, in a naive attempt to lessen his parents' suffering. Of course, he'd fail. The pain would only be transferred to the following generation.

Children are instinctively devoted and frequently relive their parents' tragedies. The family heritage can therefore become one of sorrow if these relationships of allegiance, as Hellinger describes them, are passed down over numerous generations.

4.   The child might identify with his dead brother.

The family is engulfed in sadness when a little kid passes away. The surviving sibling may even start to avoid upsetting the mourning parents by moving carefully around them. Members of the family may attempt to forget about the deceased kid and even refrain from saying his name to escape the suffering and despair of the death. By excluding the deceased kid in this manner, a favorable environment is created for an identification to flourish.

These kinds of identification have a profound impact on how our lives develop. We unknowingly and with astonishing results revisit some parts of our familial tragedies. These circumstances are not unusual. Many of us unknowingly sympathize with members of the family who have endured traumatic experiences.

The fact that the root of trauma frequently remains hidden is one of the biggest obstacles to healing from trauma. We frequently lack direction when faced with difficult emotions because we lack context for comprehending them. To free ourselves from how we may have been recreating the past, core language might reveal the trauma's source.

The process of creating your core language map involves four phases. You will receive a new tool at each stage. Each tool is designed to extract fresh data. The devices are as follows:

1.   The Core Complaint

2.   The Core Descriptors
3.   The Core Sentence
4.   The Core Trauma

Lessons

1. There is a natural flow of life that binds us with our parents. If this flow is disrupted, it greatly impacts our lives.

    - We have connected with a parent.
    - We have pushed away a parent.
    - We have suffered from a break in our early relationship with our mother.
    - We have identified with a member of our family system that is not our parents.

2. There are four common themes that disrupt the flow of life:

3. Pushing away our parents who did us wrong does not guarantee that we've escaped the cycle.

4. To understand the source of our trauma, it is important to complete our core language map, which is composed of the following: Core Complaint, Core Descriptors, Core Sentence, and Core Trauma.

Issues Surrounding the Subject Matter

1. Did you merge with the experience, feelings, or behaviors of a parent?

2. Have you rejected, blamed, judged, or cut yourself off from any of your parents?

3. Did you suffer from an interruption in the early relationship you had with your mother?

4. Are you identified with a member of your family system? Ask yourself if you have felt emotions, feelings, or behaviors that do not seem to fit in your life.

Goals

1. How is your relationship with your parents now, now that you are an adult?

2. How were your parents' lives as children? How do you think it affected them as adults?

3. How was your relationship with your mother as a child? How did you think her treatment affected your growth?

Action Steps

1. <u>Sensing the flow.</u> Take the time to feel the connection (or the lack of it) with your parents. Start by imagining your biological parents standing in front of you. (If you haven't met them, try to sense their presence and ask the following:

   - Do I welcome my parents or not?
   - Do I feel welcomed by them?
   - Do I feel differently toward one of them from the other?
   - Am I tight or relaxed as I imagine them in front of me?
   - If there is life-giving energy coming from them to me, how much will be getting through? (Answer in percentage.)

2. <u>Visualize a parent and their history</u>. For this example, we will use the father but you can do it with your mother, too. Visualize your father standing a few steps away. Imagine all the traumas he experienced or at least the brief family history you know he encountered.

   - Close your eyes and remember all of your father's familial history of tragedies.
   - Picture your father as a baby and imagine what he might have felt. Describe the sensations.

- Can you imagine the entirety of his suffering? Can you relate to it?
- Tell him in your heart, "Dad, I understand." even if you don't. Then, describe what you feel after saying it.
- How does your body react to this? Is there an area in your body that feels softer?

3. <u>Identify factors of an interrupted bond with your mother.</u> Close your eyes, again. Try to clear your mind so you can answer the questions honestly and without bias.

- Did something happen with your mother while she was carrying you in her womb?
- How was your parents' relationship during the pregnancy?
- Were you separated from your mother after your birth?
- Did your mother suffer from early interruption during the first three years of her life?
- Was your mother's attention focused on a traumatic event involving your siblings? (i.e. Miscarriage, death, stillbirth, etc.)

Checklist

1. Prepare a notebook and pen to use throughout the different exercises in the workbook.

2. It helps to know your family history, even if it's just a brief one. You need to know the basics. (Did someone in your family join the army, experience the Holocaust, be affected by the world war, etc.)

3. The journey ahead will force you to revisit the parts of your past that you might not want to. It'd be better to have someone to talk to

Part 2: The Core Language Map

Ch 6: The Core Complaint

Summary

We often convey more than we know when we discuss our anxieties and challenges. However, few of us ever consider looking there. You won't learn how to create a map of your primary languages if we never delve deeper into that portion of us. You will develop the ability to follow the trail of clues left by your words, which can take you to the source of your anxieties. We start by identifying your *core complaint*. We listen for the most intense emotional thread in the fabric of the words we utter to hear this. We pay close attention to words that have the deepest emotional resonance.

It could be something we fear or something that gives us great pain. For example, fifty-two-year-old Bob always complains, "Why does everybody leave me? Am I not good enough?" Meanwhile, Joanne's mother calls her an "abject disappointment." Joanne identified that her core complaint is that she and her mother weren't connected and that their separation and acrimonious exchanges had caused her a lot of anguish and emptiness.

We examine both our physical and somatic body language as well as our verbal language when examining the core complaint. We also pay extra attention to any symptoms or actions we exhibit that stick out as peculiar or unexpected. Twenty-six-year-old firefighter, Carson expressed his fear verbally and physically.

When he was twenty-four, he almost fell over a cliff while driving his car. Though he was able to regain control of his vehicle, he lost control over his life. He began suffering from panic attacks. His core complaints were: "I won't leave any legacy if I die. Nobody will recall me. I'll vanish entirely as if I had never been. I won't be seen favorably in the future."

It was unusual to hear from a twenty-six-year-old man who still has his whole life ahead of him. We intuitively believe the words when we look at the language of a core complaint. However, we don't always believe the context. Usually, the statements themselves are true for another person. In Carson's case, the pain belonged to his father.

After getting divorced and losing the custody battle, Carson's father has never spoken to his son again. His father felt as if he lost his legacy, his son, and that he will die without Carson knowing him. Upon realizing this, Carson made the choice to track down his father and reestablish communication. Despite having three kids with a second wife and moving out of state, his father was overjoyed to hear from Carson.

In one of the action steps below, you will try to identify your core complaint. It involves writing down all of your worries and problems until you reach the most pressing one. Remember that as you do the exercise, you should learn how to listen deeply without getting carried away with emotions.

Sandy, just like Chapter One's Gretchen, had family members who suffered during the Holocaust. When Sandy was nineteen, she suffered from extreme claustrophobia and had difficulty breathing. Her fear was, in her words, not of death itself but the knowledge of dying and not being able to do anything about it. Her core complaint goes: "I cannot breathe. I cannot get out. I will die."

Unbeknownst to her, Sandy's father was also nineteen years old when his parents and sister died from asphyxiation in a gas chamber at Auschwitz. No wonder her symptoms worsened when her father died. When she finally made the connection, Wolynn told her to visualize his deceased grandparents and aunt and talk to them.

Sandy admitted to her deceased family members that she felt their pain but that now was the time to let go of it. She acknowledged that her aunt and grandparents would not be happy that she was carrying around this pain for so long. It made Sandy tear up, especially when she felt as if love from them entered her body. Slowly, she could feel her fears go away.

Sometimes the language of our core complaint is so powerful that it compels us to dig up the family graveyards in search of solutions. However, the family history we need is frequently not easily accessible. It is doubtful that this knowledge will be spoken about at the dinner table since it is likely to be hidden in shame, shunned out of discomfort, or kept as a family secret. Sometimes we are aware of the painful past that led to our problems. But we don't always connect past events to the present.

We may use the language of our core complaint to lead us through several generations of unresolved family tension. There may be a traumatic experience that has to be recalled and investigated to be finally put to rest. Once you identify the connection you have with the past generations of the family, you can check this list by Wolynn. These are the common themes that are often repetitive in families:

Repeating language. Check if the language or words you use do not match the entirety of the context in your life. Observe if this language might belong to someone else in your family.

Repeating age. Revisit the age that you experienced this certain struggle, did it also happen to your family member when they were your age? You might find it difficult to live fully once you surpass the age of a family member who died. Or you might experience a symptom when your child reaches your age when your parent died.

Repeating symptoms, behaviors, and emotions. What triggered your symptoms or problem into motion? What happened before you experienced the issue at hand? Does it seem similar to what happened to the members of your family system?

These themes help you to unravel hidden family connections which will then lead you toward realization and healing.

Your symptom or complaint may be a creative expression helping you to finish, heal, integrate, or detach from something. These may serve as arrows guiding us in the direction of an unsolved issue. They may be able to link us with someone or something that we or our family has rejected or help reveal something to us that we are unable to notice. What's unresolved might arise when we pause and investigate them, giving our healing process a new depth. We may leave feeling more complete.

Lessons

1. The core complaint is an individual's life problem or issue.

2. The core complaint may come as a verbal statement or nonverbal gesture.

3. The core complaint we have may reflect the trauma that happened in our family's past.

4. Common themes can be found in our core complaints: repetitive language, same age, and similar symptoms, behaviors, and emotions.

Issues surrounding the subject matter

1. What problem do you have now? What is that one question that you always ask but never have the answer to?

2. Do you think the issue that you currently have is your fault? How so?

3. How does this issue affect your daily life? Does it impact your work, relationship, etc.?

Goals

1. What is your core complaint?

2. How will you generate your core language?

3. How will you identify where your core complaint originated?

Action Steps

1. Investigating your core complaint. Get your pen and notebook and do the following:

- Concentrate on the issue that is now causing you the greatest stress. It might be a problem with your career, your relationship, or your health.
- What do you wish to resolve most deeply? Perhaps you are experiencing an overwhelming challenge. You may have been experiencing this symptom or sensation your entire life.
- What change do you want to happen?
- Write what feels the most significant to you. You can include everything that comes to mind – fear or something terrible that you think might happen.
- If nothing comes to mind, answer this instead: What do you fear may happen to you if the sensation, symptom, or ailment you have never gone away?
- After writing your answers, read them without feeling anything. Remember that you are seeking a language that is unusual to you.
- Reread them one more time, but let yourself feel the emotions they awaken in you this time. Ask yourself what words may not fit in the context of your life experience.

2. <u>Ask yourself these questions that will help generate your core language.</u> Write the first answer that comes to mind; that should be your final answer. Do not edit or sabotage yourself, or modify your initial thoughts to fit an outcome that you want. Let your answers flow honestly.

- What was going on in your life at the time your symptom or issue first manifested?
- At what age did the condition or issue first manifest? Did someone in your family have a traumatic event at a similar age?
- What precisely occurs in the issue?
- What are you unable to perform as a result of the issue or symptom? What does it need of you?
- What could be the worst thing that might happen to you if the sensation or symptom persisted?

3. <u>Compare answers to the repeating themes listed above.</u> Read what you've written from Action Plan #2. As you read your answers, revisit the list of common themes found in families if you recognize anything similar.

Checklist

1. Look for context clues. In the previous chapter's checklist, you were asked to learn a brief history of your family. Now, bring it out to connect the dots between their past and your present.

2. Have the list of common family themes ready. A memory might come up when you're no longer writing down answers, you must still be able to note this observation.

3. Do not edit your answers to the questions above and to the following chapters. You must write the first thing that comes to mind.

Ch 7: Core Descriptors

Summary

We can gain insight into who we are by how we feel about our parents. They also provide access to the four underlying themes that were first mentioned in chapter 5 and allow us to identify which ones are present in our daily lives. You'll be prompted to give an open and honest description of your biological parents in the future. Please skip this chapter if you have never met your biological parents.

Take time to write down adjectives to describe your parents and you can also include your partners, close friends, boss, or anyone close to you. These adjectives provide access to our repressed emotions. They may expose sentiments we may not even be conscious we have regarding our parents. We are given the chance to skip the adult-rationalized, perfected version of our childhood tale by making an unplanned list of descriptors and phrases. Our actual opinions can be shown in this writing without the normal censors and filters.

This list might help us discover any unspoken allegiances or alliances we may have with our parents. Additionally, it might show how we abandoned either or both of our parents or how we have taken on the very traits we find objectionable in them. These descriptions are truthful because they originate from an inner image that we hold and that was possibly developed long ago to save us from experiencing harm.

Many of us have sad memories of our parents not providing us with enough or not receiving the help we needed. If left unchecked, these inner perceptions have the power to determine how our lives develop, acting as a blueprint for our future selves. Additionally, these pictures are lacking and were potent enough to stop the flow of love in our family; what horrific events lie behind them?

If we didn't get along with our folks, our core descriptions will reveal whatever grudges we may still be holding. Our inner tranquility suffers when we are resentful. People who believe they did not receive enough from their parents, particularly their moms, frequently believe they do not receive enough from life.

Our fundamental adjectives show the compassion and warmth we have for our parents when we have a close relationship with them. When we have favorable feelings about our parents, we often have positive feelings about life in general and have faith that positive times will continue to happen for us.

Look at this example where two sisters describe their mother:

Eldest Daughter: Frustrated, lonely, sad, strict, and violent; she used to have a bad temper.

Youngest Daughter: Cruel, emotionally abusive, and vindictive.

According to Wolynn, the eldest daughter shows the description as a truth. No judgments have been made. Meanwhile, with the youngest sister, it is visible that her issue was not yet resolved. We can live in peace with a mother who is aggressive and has a nasty temper. The second sister is not okay with her mother since she perceives her to be purposely unkind.

One can only speculate on how the two sisters had quite different life experiences. Each sister had a unique inner representation of their mother. The second sister's life was lived as harsh and cruel. She spent a lot of time alone and felt emotionally depleted and unsupported.

Many of us struggle to find tranquility and a sense of firm ground under our feet because we suffered an early separation from or a rupture in the link with our mother. Here are some core descriptors from those who experienced an early break in their connection with their mothers:

- *Mom was aloof and cold. Never did she hold me. I had zero faith in her.*
- *I'm incredibly close with my mother. She is like my younger sister whom I look after.*
- *My mother was judgmental, aloof, and incapable of showing emotion.*
- *My mother and I don't have a relationship.*
- *She made me feel afraid. I was never sure of what might come next.*

It's crucial to understand that not all people who have had a break in their mother-child relationship will harbor bitterness toward her. In other cases, the rupture happened so young in life that no cognitive recall of the event remains. However, when connection or distance has occurred in partnerships, body memories of the distance may be evoked. We can experience a wave of alienation, annihilation, disconnection, defeat, and numbness without ever understanding why.

Your core descriptions' emotional content might serve as a barometer to determine how much healing is still required. In general, the direction of healing is obvious the deeper the negative charge. You're searching for words with a strong emotional impact. Keep in mind that your sorrow will be more intense the more emotionally charged your remarks are.

When a parent is disregarded or rejected, one of the kids will frequently act in ways that reflect the disregarded parent. In doing so, the kid equalizes himself or herself to the parent by experiencing equivalent anguish. We must resolve our differences with our parents. By doing this, we not only find inner serenity, but we also enable harmony to permeate the succeeding generations.

To repair your connection with your parents, your fundamental descriptions are an important first step. No matter if your parents are still alive or have passed away, once you unlock your core descriptors, the unfavorable attitudes, judgments, and thoughts you have about them can finally change. You cannot alter who your parents are, but you can shift how you view them.

Lessons

1. What we feel about our parents say a lot about our identity and our past.

2. The core descriptors are the words or phrases of adjectives we use to describe our parents.

3. Our core descriptors show whether we have accepted our parents or not. It shows how much healing is needed.

4. Changing the image we have of our parents helps in our healing process.

Issues surrounding the subject matter

1. Why do you think it's important to know how you think of your parents?

2. What is the worst thing that you're parents have done to you? Or what is it in your childhood that brought you the most trauma?

3. Do you agree that your relationship with your parents can affect your romantic relationships?

Goals

1. How would you describe your mother? How did she treat you as a child?

2. Likewise, how would you describe your father? How was your relationship with him as his kid?

3. How would you describe the people close to you? Does it reflect the same idea as how you'd describe your parents?

Action Steps

1. <u>Describe your mother</u>. Write what you think about your mother. Just like the previous activity, it should be the first thing that comes to mind. Don't read it after, just write them all down. Complete the sentence "My mother was..." And if applicable, also write what you blame her for.

2. <u>Describe your father.</u> Do the same thing for your father following the instructions above. Again, do not read it after writing. Just keep the flow going.

3. <u>Describe your close friend, boss, or partner.</u> This is optional but if you feel like they do have a big role to play in what is happening in your life, it is suggested that you include them. Again, do not stop to read.

4. <u>Alter the inner image you have of your parents.</u> Now, read your core descriptors aloud. Relate your descriptors to the explanations given in the chapter summary. It's time to shift your perception of your parents. Ask yourself the following questions:
   - Open your mind and listen carefully. Do you hear something different?
   - Do the strong statements suggest that you still harbor resentment toward your parents?
   - As you study the descriptions, feel your body. Does your body tense up or loosen up? How's your breathing? Is it moving or halted?
   - Look inside yourself to see if anything wants to change.

Checklist

1. You might not like it but it will help to have a picture of your parents when you were still young. Or better, if it's a family picture including you as a kid. Photos, or memories, in general, bring out the most vulnerable emotions and thoughts.

2. Write what comes first to your mind, do not put too much thought into how you formulated the words.

3. Be honest with yourself. Do not use sugarcoated words as core descriptors, regardless of how harsh your final words will be.

Ch 8: The Core Sentence

If you have anxiety, panic attacks, or intrusive thoughts, you are all too familiar with what it's like to be imprisoned in the cage of your inner existence. Even if there has never been a trial or conviction, the difficult period you experience inside yourself might appear like a life sentence. That lifestyle may be draining. It's easier than you think to escape. You just have to serve a new sort of "life sentence"—the one that your darkest fear imposes—to "do time."

"Do time." You've probably known this short sentence since you were a little child. This phrase, whether stated aloud or silently, makes you feel even more hopeless. However, it can also help you escape from your cage and enter a new realm of comprehension and resolve. Your core sentence is this particular phrase. If the core language map is an instrument for seeking hidden riches, the core sentence is the gem you discover once you arrive.

Later on, you will be asked to identify your greatest fear and thus produce your core sentence. There will be prompts to guide you to narrow it down. But what do you do when nothing comes to you? Answer this question: "What's the worst thing that could happen to someone else?" Perhaps you might recall reading in the news about a horrific incident involving a stranger or someone you know. Anything you recall is crucial.

Even so, it may reveal something about you because most of the time, someone else's tragedy might reflect our fears.

Another way to identify your core sentence is to think of a part from a play, book, or movie that greatly impacted you. What portion of that scene has the biggest impact on you? What aspect of a narrative about youngsters who are all by themselves without their mother, for instance, connects with you the most? Is it because a mother abandoned her kids? Or is it the idea that no one is there to watch over the kids and they are left alone?

This is similar to what happened with Pam who had this fear of someone entering her home and harming her. However, this fear had been hidden in her mind for quite some time until she heard the news of a Somalian boy who died from being brutally beaten by a local gang. Pam said, "He wasn't guilty. He was simply in the wrong place at the wrong time by accident. They snatched his life and his dignity from him. They caused him pain."

Unknowingly, Pam was referring to Walter, her mother's brother, who died when he was only eleven years old. Pam's family had suspected foul play, that Walter was tricked by his bullies, which is why his body was found at the abandoned mine shaft. Pam only heard the story once but it stuck with her all these years.

The past frequently remains buried in families who have gone through traumatic or upsetting situations. Parents frequently keep their mouths shut because they believe it's preferable to spare their kids any needless suffering. Unfortunately, not talking about the past doesn't do anything to protect the next generation. What is hidden from view and the mind seldom vanishes. On the other hand, it frequently recurs in our children's actions and symptoms.

Let us revisit Gretchen's case from Chapter One. Her core language was: "I want to vaporize myself. My body will be incinerated in merely seconds." Besides identifying with her grandmother who had her whole family incinerated, Gretchen also identified with the people who hurt her family. Wolynn said this is usual since the perpetrators are also part of the family system.

Gretchen was asked to visualize that she was being comforted by her grandmother and her Jewish family members whom she never had a chance to meet. Gretchen felt a warm, peaceful feeling as she did so. At that moment, she had no desire to kill herself. She no longer felt the need to do it.

Even though many of us do not have family members who died or participated in the world's greatest tragedies like the Holocaust, the Killing Fields of Cambodia, the Armenian genocide, the Stalin-imposed Ukrainian famine, or the mass killings in various countries, there are remnants of exile, murder, oppression, forced relocation, rape, violence, war, and other such traumas that our ancestors endured can contribute to the fears and anxieties we thought originated with us.

Core sentences frequently evoke emotions and physical manifestations of fear. We can feel our body react physically strongly only by saying its words. Many claim that when the statement is pronounced, waves of sensation reverberate within them. Because of an unsolved tragedy, a core sentence is born. The next question is whose is it?

Zach always thought that he needed to die. In his desire to succeed, he tried to do it in bizarre ways. For one, he enlisted in the army intending to be killed in Iraq but their unit was never deployed. Next, he drove down a busy highway at a very high speed, hoping that a state trooper would stop and pull him over. Then, he would attempt to steal the trooper's gun and in self-defense, he would shoot Zach. But again, no chase happened.

His third plan included carrying a toy gun toward the president's office, assuming someone in the Secret Service would kill him on sight. But when he arrived, the security was so tight that he did not even make it near the gate. We can see that all of his suicide attempts involved dying for the country, in some ways.

Wolynn gave Zach three bridging questions, which are as follows:

- Who in your family had committed a crime and yet received no punishment?

- Who thought he deserved to be shot for something they did?
- Who in your family was shot and the family was unable to grieve?

It turned out that the first two questions hit a bull's eye. Zach's grandfather was an official in Mussolini's cabinet. He was in charge of making decisions that killed countless people. But before he got caught, he was able to change his name and escape to the US. The rest of the cabinet members died at the hands of a firing squad. The grandfather thought he had been lucky, but the guilt was passed down to his grandson.

When the old sentiments surfaced, Zach had a plan. In his mind's eye, he would visualize his grandfather and bow respectfully. He'd hear his grandfather tell him that the desire to die was his, that he'd manage it, and Zach could simply breathe freely and be at ease. Zach envisioned his grandfather making apologies to those he had wronged in the afterlife. The entire scene began to take on a serene, reconciling tone in Zach's mind.

Repeat your core sentence to yourself. Take a moment to consider that the words are not your own. To better perceive the words presented to you, you might even wish to rewrite your core sentence. Hear the sentencing of someone who endured severe trauma, who harbored intense anguish or remorse, who passed away brutally or regrettably, or who led a life of emptiness or silent despair. But now, the pain lives in you.

We seem to have an unspoken responsibility to make amends for the catastrophes of our family history. These words have an impact on how you perceive yourself. They have an impact on your decisions. They have an impact on how your body and mind react to the environment. One more time, state your thesis statement and ponder: Are you certain that this dread comes from you? Is there a member in your family system that had a similar emotion?

Your core sentence—the one that expresses your greatest fear—is the most effective strategy you will learn in this book for locating unresolved familial trauma. It not only directs you to the cause of your anxiety but also links you to any residual feelings of unresolved familial trauma. The terror might start to fade when the source is seen.

Here are some attributes of a core sentence:

1. It frequently refers to a painful incident in your family's past or from your youth.
2. It mostly starts with a "They" or "I" sentence.
3. It's a dramatic, short sentence.
4. It uses the very emotive language of your worst fear.
5. Speaking makes you physically react.

6. It can find the place in your family background where a language first appeared and recover the "lost language" of a tragedy.
7. It can bring back traumatic memories that were lost.
8. It might provide you perspective for comprehending the feelings and sensations you've been having.
9. It tackles the root problem rather than the symptoms.
10. Speaking it out loud might help you let go of the past.

Lessons

1. The core sentence is used to identify our greatest fear; it shows our most vulnerable emotions and dramatic thoughts.

2. There are many ways to discover your core sentences. You just have to dig a little deeper.

3. Identifying your core sentence is the most effective way of identifying the source of your family trauma.

Issues surrounding the subject matter

1. What is your greatest fear? Is this fear acquired or has it developed at some point?

2. Did an event, incident, or factor trigger this fear to unlock?

3. How do you deal with your fear? Do you embrace it or attempt to run away from it?

Goals

1. How are you going to generate your core sentence?

2. How are you going to acknowledge the family members that have caused you the trauma you suffer from?

3. Moving forward, how are you going to deal with this fear?

Action Steps

1. <u>Identify your core sentence.</u> Complete the statement: "My worst fear, the worst thing that could happen to me, is..." Answer this first before moving on to the next part of the action steps.

2. <u>Tweak your core sentence.</u> Complete the sentences below based on the sentence you formulated earlier.

   - "I..."
   - "They..."
   - "I could..."
   - "My spouse/family/children could..."

3. Deepen your core sentence. Complete the statement: "My absolute worst fear is..."

4. Link your core sentence to the source. Identify which family member has experienced the one thing you are scared of. Acknowledge their experience.

Checklist

1. Revisit books or movies that impacted you greatly. Look for which scene of the film or novel has particularly struck a chord. This could be where your greatest fear lies.

2. Think back to a certain event or piece of news you've watched, heard of, or read that triggered a fear you did not use to have.

3. In your notebook, paste a cutout of the list of ten key attributes of a core sentence or write them down. Use it as a guide as you work on identifying your core sentence.

Ch 9: The Core Trauma

Summary

We've mastered the art of separating our *core complaint* and *core language*. As part of our analysis of our *core descriptors*, we discovered that the adjectives we choose to characterize our parents frequently reveal more about ourselves than they do about them. We also discovered that the statement that best captures our *core sentence* can take us back to a traumatic event in our family system. Building a bridge to our *core trauma*—the unresolved trauma from childhood or family history—is the last skill we need to acquire.

As in the previous chapter, we learned from Zach that we can use bridging questions to uncover an underlying trauma. It could help bring a family member to mind, one from whom we have acquired our core sentence. Since our core sentence may have originated in a previous generation, discovering the true owner can provide serenity and understanding not only to ourselves but also to our offspring.

Lisa described herself as an overprotective mother. She was terrified that something terrible would happen to one of her children, so she never let them out of her sight. Even though nothing significant had ever happened to any of Lisa's three children, she was haunted by her core sentence, "My child will die." Lisa knew very little about her family history, but when she followed the fear of her core sentence, she listed the bridging questions below:

- *Which member of the family had children who died?*
- *Which member of the family could not keep their children safe?*

Lisa's sole knowledge was that her ancestors immigrated to America from Ukraine's Carpathian Mountains region. Her grandparents fled hunger and destitution and never spoke about their sufferings. Lisa's mother was the youngest among the siblings and the only one born in the United States. Although Lisa's mother was unsure of the specifics, she assumed that some of the children died on the voyage.

Lisa's knowledge of her anxiety grew simply by bringing this information to light. She recognized the phrase "My kid will die" as belonging to her grandparents. This allowed her to let go and enabled her children enjoy life a little more. When you address your bridging questions, you can come face to face with a tragic incident in your family that has never properly healed. You may find yourself in the presence of family members who have endured great difficulties.

Another way to unearth unresolved family trauma is to create a genogram. It is a two-dimensional depiction of a family tree. Here are the instructions on how to create one:

1. Make a diagram of your family's three or four generations back, including your great-grandparents, grandparents, parents, uncles, aunts, and siblings. You don't have to go any further back than your great-grandparents. Create a family tree by using squares to indicate men and circles to indicate females.

2. Write down the key traumas and tough destinies that each family member has endured. If your parents are still living, you might ask them for information. Don't be concerned if you can't receive answers. Anything you know should be enough

3. Write your core statement at the top of the genogram. Take a look at everyone in your family system. Who else might have had the same feelings you do? Often, it is a person who is not often discussed in your family. Remember to create a different genogram for your maternal family line and another for your paternal family line.

As an example, let's take a peek into Carole's life. She has been overweight since she turned eleven. When she reached the age of thirty-eight, she had gained more weight. She used the words "suffocated and smothered" to describe her weight and that she felt like her body had betrayed her. She further narrated that she developed earlier than most girls her age. When she got her period at eleven, she started hating her body.

On top of that, her greatest fear is that she'd be alone without someone.

Carole's core language map looks like this:

Core Complaint: My weight suffocates and smothers me. My body betrayed me.

Core Sentence: I will be alone without somebody.

Bridging Questions:

- Who among her family members feels deceived by their body?
- Who was suffocated and/or smothered?
- Which family member felt deceived by her womb?
- Which family member suffered a horrible tragedy due to, during, or in the aftermath of pregnancy?
- Who has ever felt completely alone in the absence of others?

Now, for the core trauma, let us revisit Carole's history. Carole's grandmother had three children: two boys and a girl – Carole's mother. During the delivery, both boys got suffocated in the grandmother's birth canal, which resulted in the boys becoming mentally handicapped. The boys, Carole's uncles, had been living in their mother's basement for fifty years. With what we know, we can make the connection that Carole's complaint came from this incident.

Further, Carole also began hating her body when she got her period, which is when her body can now conceive a child. She isolated herself because of this self-hatred. Her grandmother also lived a solitary life and died in isolation, the same way her uncles did. Not to mention Carole's mother who also felt alone her whole life – having her mother focus on her brothers and trapped in her sadness.

Her entire body began to shake as she realized she had been bearing the family's agony for her grandmother, uncles, and mother. An emotional weight was lifted, allowing her to inhabit parts of herself that had previously been shut down. It wouldn't be long before Carole had physical knowledge of her body, allowing her to make various lifestyle choices.

Having the connection to your familial history within reach, the only thing left to do is bring what you've found back to yourself. What has gone unsaid or unnoticed in your family history is most likely lurking in the depths of your self-awareness. When you make the connection, what was previously overlooked might become a healing opportunity. Sometimes new visuals demand our attention and care to completely incorporate them.

<u>Lessons</u>

1. The core trauma is the last part of the core language map. This is where we pinpoint the source of the trauma you are carrying.

2. Bridging questions are derived from the core sentences and it assists us in narrowing down the cause of your core complaint.

3. A genogram is a visual tool that can be used to oversee the history of an individual family member of up to three generations.

Issues Surrounding the Subject Matter

1. Based on your core sentence, what are the words that make sense to you? What are those that do not?

2. Why do you think it's important to ask bridging questions?

3. Are you open to knowing the source of your core sentence? Why or why not?

4. How do you think you would feel if you were to find out the truth about your trauma?

Goals

1. How are you going to form bridging questions from your core sentence?

2. How will you know the source of your core trauma?

3. How are you going to complete your core language map?

Action Steps

1. <u>Identify bridging questions from your core sentence.</u> Write it down as follows:
   - My Core Sentence:
   - My Bridging Questions:

2. Create a genogram of your family. Refer to the instructions in the chapter summary. Create one for your mother's side and one for your father's side.

3. After you create your genogram, analyze the connection of everything in your life and update your core language map. It should look like this:

   - My Core Complaint:
   - My Core Descriptors (both parents):
   - My Core Sentence:
   - My Bridging Questions:
   - My Core Trauma

Checklist

1. If you are married or with a serious partner, you can ask them to create a genogram for their family. It'll help you

pinpoint the source of your problems that may affect your relationship.

2. At this point, a brief history of the family may not be enough. It helps if you can research deeper using the bridging questions.

3. Open your mind to learning about your family, regardless of how hard it may seem. It'll bring you a healing opportunity.

Part 3: Pathways to Reconnection

Ch 10: From Insight to Integration

Summary

We are related to persons in our family background whose repressed traumas have become our inheritance. When the link is unconscious, we might be trapped in memories and experiences from the past. With our family history in mind, however, the paths toward freedom are clear.

Sometimes simply connecting our situation to an underlying trauma in our history is sufficient. Carole's knowledge alone was powerful enough to cause a strong reaction she could feel in her heart. For some of us, becoming conscious of what transpired in our families must be followed with an activity or experience that results in a release or more ease in our body.

At this point in your journey, you have already gained knowledge of the sentences and words that are most likely not yours. It's time to bring the different pieces of the puzzle together. Here is a summary of what we have discussed:

- Core Complaint - the core language that describes your worst complaint, worry, or struggle
- Core Descriptors - the core language that describes your parents
- Core Sentence - the core language that refers to your greatest fear
- Core Trauma - the event or events in your family that causes your core language

Family trauma can pass down indefinitely. But we have the power to stop the recurring cycle once we acknowledge that we have been harboring emotions, thoughts, sensations, behaviors, or illnesses that did not begin with us. We begin by consciously acknowledging the awful occurrence and the persons affected. Often, this starts with an internal discussion or a conversation with a family member, either in person or by imagination. The correct words may free us from unconscious familial bonds and allegiance, as well as break the cycle of inherited pain.

We need to make peace with our trauma by creating personal healing sentences. Here are some examples from Wolynn's clients:

A man who shared the loneliness and isolation of his grandfather said: *I, too, have felt lonely and alone. I realize that this is not even mine. I understand that this is not what you choose for me. And I understand it pains you to watch me suffer in this way. From now on, I shall live my life close to the people surrounding me. I'll honor you in this way.*

Another woman, carrying her grandmother and mother's unhappiness and failed relationships said: *Mom, please provide me with the ability to be content with my spouse even though you couldn't be joyful with Dad. To respect you and Dad, I will enjoy my love with my spouse so that you both may see how great things are going for me.*

A young lady bearing the pain and anxiousness of her mother who died during her delivery said: *Whenever I feel nervous, I see you beaming at me, encouraging me, and wishing me well. I'll sense you here with me every time I experience my breath flowing inside me, and I'll know you're glad for me.*

You might have already sensed a new internal sensation taking root when writing your healing lines. It may have occurred to you as an image or an emotion, or as a sense of connection or belongingness. Perhaps you sensed the compassion of family members gazing over you. Perhaps you had a better feeling of serenity as if something unsolved was finally being resolved.

All of these events can have a significant impact on recovery. Essentially, they provide an inner context of feeling whole, which we may return to if previous sentiments threaten our stability. Through exercises, practice, and ritual, these new memories and visions continue to deepen. Here are some examples you can get an idea from:

Place a photo on the desk.

A man who realized he was reliving his grandpa's guilt displayed a portrait of his grandpa on his table. He imagined leaving his guilt emotions with his granddad. He felt better and happier each time he performed this ritual.

Light a candle.

A lady unwittingly shared her father's estrangement from the family when she was twenty-nine, the same age his father died. For two months, she lit a candle every night and envisioned the flame burning an opening for the two of them to reconcile. She would talk to her father and experience his calming presence. Her unpleasant sentiments had subsided by the end of the ritual, and she was filled with fresh warm ones.

Write a letter.

A man who suddenly left his college fiancee found it hard to find happiness in his relationships twenty years later. He found out that the woman he left died a year after the separation. Despite knowing she wouldn't receive the letter, he still wrote one, saying: "I apologize for hurting you. I understand it was terrible for you, I'm sorry. I will never have the chance to send this letter but I hope you receive my sincere words." Afterward, he felt a strange sense of peace.

Place a photo above the bed.

A woman realized that her early separation from her mother affected how she had treated her. Her barriers relaxed as she hung a picture of her mother on the wall over her pillow and requested her mother to cuddle her every night while she slept. She could imagine her mother touching her as she lay in bed. Her mother's love, she said, was like a surge of electricity that brought her courage. By the end of the year, she could physically sense her mother's support for her throughout the day.

Create a boundary.

A woman grew up carrying the burden of making her alcoholic mother happy and well. This was reflected in her future relationships as an adult. In her room, she created a circle around her using yarn. She told her mother: "This is my space. My feelings are over here and your feelings are over there. I would have done everything to make you happy as a kid but it's too much now. I will honor my feelings so I will not lose myself when I get connected with somebody"

The practices and rituals mentioned may seem insignificant in comparison to the enormous sorrow one has been carrying for years, but research shows that the more we revisit and repeat these new images and sensations, the more they merge inside us. Furthermore, when we envision a soothing image, we engage the same brain areas connected with emotions of well-being and pleasant emotion.

Our capacity to integrate the experiences of our bodily senses into the healing process is critical. In the effort to understand ourselves, we often get insight when we are ready to accept what is difficult. Consider chatting to a small child who feels invisible and unheard. There is probably a child there—a part of you that has been neglected for a long time. Consider that this little one has been yearning for you to acknowledge them for a long time, and this is the day.

Here are some healing sentences we can tell ourselves:

- *I am here for you.*
- *I will hold you tight.*
- *I've got you always.*
- *I will comfort you.*
- *I will be here even when you're overwhelmed and scared.*
- *I will stay with you.*

We comfort the parts of us that feel most delicate when we lay our hands on our bodies and channel our thoughts and breath inside. In doing so, we have the opportunity to alleviate or release what we perceive to be intolerable. As the new sentiments take root, we may notice that we feel more protected in our bodies.

When we harbor negative thoughts and emotions towards our parents, we also feel the repercussions within us. We may not know it, but pushing our father or mother away is equivalent to pushing a part of ourselves away. When we distance ourselves from our parents, the bad traits we see in them might manifest in us unknowingly. The solution is to discover a means to allow our parents into our hearts and bring to light the things we despise in them (and in ourselves).

Healing can take place even though they have died, are in jail, or are drowning in agony. Allowing yourself to engage with a pleasant inner image might start to transform the way you interact with your parents on the outside. You can't alter what happened, but you can repair what is, as long as you don't anticipate your parents to change or become anything other than who they are.

Reconciliation is primarily an interior process. Our connection with our parents is not determined by what they do, who they are, or how they react. It all comes down to what we do. Change occurs inside us.

Here are some healing sentences we can say when we have rejected a parent:

- *I apologize that I have distanced myself so much.*
- *Every time you have reached out, I have always pushed you away.*
- *This is not easy to admit but I miss you.*
- *I'm sorry for being difficult to deal with.*
- *I apologize for being judgmental, it hindered me from building a relationship with you.*

Before attempting to mend a badly damaged connection with your parents, you may want to first consult with a body-centered therapist or establish a guided meditation practice to discover tools that will help you to connect with your body's sensations. It is critical for you to develop an inner sense that both directs and supports you.

For those who can no longer physically connect with their parents because of death, remember that you still have your inner connection with them. Here are some healing statements you can use:

- *Please comfort me in my sleep when I'm easier to reach.*
- *Please tell me how to trust someone else and let genuine love in.*
- *Please support me in finding peace within my body.*

When a parent abandons us or gives us up to be fostered by others, the anguish may be unbearable. In a way, the initial departure creates an unconscious pattern for the numerous abandonments and rejections that happen later in our lives. We're prone to repeat the cycle as long as we persist to believe we've been wronged or harmed.

Here are some statements you can use to imagine saying to your estranged parent:

- *I understand if leaving or giving me away made life easier for you.*

- *I'm going to quit accusing you, which I realize is simply holding us both prisoner.*
- *I'll gather what I require from other people and make the most of a bad situation.*
- *What transpired between us will be a source of strength for me.*
- *Thank you for giving me life. I swear not to squander or waste it.*

While some of us reject our parents, others integrate with them in ways that muddle our identity and diminish our uniqueness. If this is the case for you, you may read the following phrases as if you were hearing them from your father or mother:

- *I appreciate you for who you are. You don't have to do anything to earn my affection.*
- *I've been too near to you, and I realize how much it's cost you.*
- *My requirements made it impossible for you to make time for yourself.*
- *I was too near to you to enable you to recognize yourself. Now I'll just sit here and enjoy observing you live your life.*
- *I will be content if you take a moment to pause till you can feel the flow of your own life through you.*

If you've followed the procedures in this section, you may have already noticed a new form of inner calm. The healing phrases you've uttered, as well as the exercises, pictures, practices, and rituals you've experienced, may have aided in the strengthening of a relationship with a loved one or the relief of an underlying attachment to a family member.

Lessons

1. We need to acknowledge our family's past and make peace with it to stop the cycle. Otherwise, we might pass it on to the next generation

2. We do not have to meet with the family members to find closure, it is enough to tell them that we understand.

3. Having a healing ritual or practice allows us to integrate our learning into action.

Issues Surrounding the Subject Matter

1. Why is it important to accept your family's past?

2. How will you deal with everything that you've gained so far?

3. How do you think you will move forward after acknowledging your family history?

Goals

1. How are you going to make peace with your past?

2. How will you feel after making peace with your family history?

3. How are you going to find closure with your trauma?

Action Steps

1. <u>Make peace with your family history</u>. Follow the instructions below:

   - Write the core language with the most dramatic feeling and the tragedy (or tragedies) that are linked to this.
   - Make a list of the individuals who were impacted by these tragic events. Include all family and non-family members.
   - In vivid words, describe the event that took place.
   - Observe if the visual affects your body in some way. If it feels like it's drawing to a specific part of your body, put your hand there and breathe.
   - Imagine the people who are part of this event, talk to them. Let them know that they are important and that you will do something special to honor their existence.

2. Write down your healing sentences toward these people. You can use the above examples as a guide.

3. Start a routine or practice that will aid your self-healing. Refer to the examples above.

Checklist

1. You can prepare a photo of your family members that are affected by the trauma if they are no longer alive. You can address them as if you're speaking to them directly.

2. If you opt to write a letter as a self-healing exercise, you can also burn it afterward. It will be as if you're also releasing the trauma that was handed down to you.

3. You can search for other activities for self-healing. It could be something that only you and this family member can relate to. You can make it more personal.

Ch 11: The Core Language of Separation

Summary

Some core languages do not come from previous generations. It is possible that those were developed when we were separated from our mother right after we were born. Remember that we discussed how our life is handed down by our parents in a blueprint. This blueprint starts within our mother's womb which means that at this moment, our whole world is our mother. This carries over and persists even after we are born, making us crave her smell, gaze, and touch.

Through the gentleness of her care and presence, when our mother is attuned to us, she gives us a sense of belonging and security. She suffuses us with all her "good things," and we grow an internal "happy feeling" reserve as a result. To believe that the wonderful feeling will stay inside of us even when we briefly lose our way, we need to accumulate enough "good things" in our reservoir throughout our formative years.

When we have enough of the "good stuff," a simple interruption will not bother us. However, if there is not enough "good stuff" and our bond with our mother gets interrupted, we will no longer be able to trust our mommies. And since, during this time, our mother is our whole world, we also lose trust in life itself.

However, when the early relationship with our mother is broken, a gloomy atmosphere of dread, scarcity, and distrust may take over as our default state. The distance between mother and child can become a foundation for many of life's difficulties, regardless of whether this break in the relationship is permanent or not. When this connection is broken, it feels like we are cut off from life.

When the split is brief, our mother must continue to welcome us when we get back together. Because of how upsetting it might be to lose her, we may be reluctant or resistant to getting in touch with her again. She may never comprehend why she feels alienated from us and why we continue to struggle with emotions of inadequacy, disappointment, and uncertainty about her capacity to raise us.

Since we cannot remember these events as memories, they could most likely reveal themselves as cravings or needs when we reach adulthood. This is why sometimes we tend to look for our parents' qualities in our romantic partners. As a result, we either stick to our spouse as we may have done with our mother, or we push them away in fear of losing closeness. Our spouse may feel imprisoned on a never-ending emotional roller coaster when we frequently exhibit both traits in the same relationship.

There are several types of separation. The physical kinds include adoption, illnesses and hospitalizations, work, birth complications, and long trips away from your home. Any of these can endanger bond development between a child and its mother. But emotional separations are also another aspect. This is when the mother is physically present but still fails to connect with the child.

The above types all happen after the child is born but some disconnections happen when the child is still in its mother's womb. The triggers could include a stressful relationship with a partner, the death of a beloved, depression, fear, or anxiety. But do not lose hope. When you have grown into an adult, you can still reconnect with your parents. The first step is to identify your core language.

Here are some examples of core sentences from people who had experienced early separation from their mothers:

- *I will be left behind.*
- *People will reject me.*
- *I will have nobody.*
- *I do not matter in this world.*
- *I am too much.*
- *They will hurt and betray me.*

A deep rejection of our mothers paired with a sense of guilt over her inability to care for us is a typical element that marks an early separation. But this isn't always the case. Even though we might have never truly bonded with our mothers, we might still feel a deep affection for her and a sense of responsibility to take better care of her. The path of tending might change due to our desire to feel a connection to her.

Wanda was a depressed sixty-two-year-old woman. Suffering from alcohol addiction and going through three divorces, she was alone and never felt peace in her life. When asked to describe her mother, she used the words "aloof, cold, and distant." But when we look deeper into Wanda's story, we will understand why.

Evelyn, Wanda's mother, fell asleep while taking care of her first-born daughter. She accidentally rolled over baby Gail and killed her. In an attempt to soothe the grief within them, Evelyn and her husband made love and conceived Wanda. But for Evelyn, the guilt never left. She distanced herself from Wanda to attempt to protect her daughter, not knowing that this behavior led to Wanda's destruction.

Wanda didn't realize that her mother's aloofness wasn't personal and was instead related to Gail's passing sixty years ago. She had spent her whole childhood hating and accusing her mother of failing to show her enough affection. As Wanda made the connection, she left Wolynn's office and rushed home. She said to Wolynn that she had to tell her mother how much she loves her as she is running out of time.

In the womb, we form our first ideas about who we are and the way our lives will go. Our basic personality is influenced by our mother's emotions throughout pregnancy, which may either make us peaceful or agitated, responsive or rebellious, resilient or rigid. When something happens that disrupts the important bond, we feel emptiness and pain. This disconnects us from the flow of life.

The worst-case scenarios include the possibility of children becoming sociopaths and psychopaths. As Carole McKelvey and Dr. Ken Magid wrote in their book *High Risk: Children Without a Conscience,* "All of us have the same energy of rage. But the rage of psychopaths is rooted from unresolved needs as infants." These severe situations highlight how important it is for mothers or other early caregivers to shape a child's compassion, understanding, as well as respect for oneself, others, and all of life.

Many of us have suffered from minor interruptions from the early bond with our mothers. The fact is that a mother can't be 100% attuned to her children all the time. But sometimes, these minor separations help the children grow to be independent, provided that they work together to reconnect. Repairing a connection regularly fosters trust and promotes a safe bond between mother and child.

Lessons

1. We developed certain core languages when we were momentarily or permanently separated from our mothers after being born.

2. If our mother had given us enough attention and care, temporary separation would not greatly affect us.

3. We have needs as children and when not met, these will manifest as cravings when we become adults.

Issues Surrounding the Subject Matter

1. How do you view your life at the moment?

2. Is your view of life as an adult similar to your view of your mother as a kid?

3. Did you have a good relationship with your mother as a child?

Goals

1. How are you going to link your childhood struggles to your adulthood problems?

2. How would it feel if you were able to identify the connection between the past to the present?

3. How will you envision your life after making peace with your childhood separation?

Action Steps

1. Revisit your earliest childhood memory.

   - Is your mother present in the picture?
   - How did you feel?
   - What were you doing?
   - How is your relationship with your mother?

2. Identify the similarities between your childhood and how you view life at the present.

   - Would you use the same words to describe both childhood and adulthood?
   - What are you craving? Is it something you didn't have enough of or were denied as a child?
   - Look for any connection that could be made.

3. Go back to your core sentence. Identify what kind of separation from the parent it belongs to.

Checklist

1. Look at your baby pictures. Feel the emotions of each photo, remember what happened, and let it take you back to the past. It will help you become more aware of how you were feeling back then.

2. Go back to your core language map and recheck if any of the words you used might be directly related to early separation.

3. Tell your mother how much you love her or how much you appreciate her.

Ch 12: The Core Language of Relationships

Summary

Sometimes, despite how hard we try to break the cycle of failed relationships in our family, we tend to get trapped in it. This is because of how love is portrayed in the previous generations of our families. However, most problems encountered in relationships do not belong in the present relationship itself. Rather, it stems from the family dynamics we have unconsciously inherited.

At first glance, Dan and Nancy would seem like a successful married couple who had fully lived their life. Nancy was a hospital administrator while Dan was a CEO of a well-established financial institution. They have three college-educated children who are doing well. But when you look more closely, Dan and Nancy are not happy with their marriage. Let us take a good look at their core languages. We need to ask the following questions to identify the couple's core language map.

Core Complaint: What is the biggest complaint you have against your partner?

111

Identifying the couple's core complaints was easy. Having attended tons of couple counseling, the words came freely. Nancy claimed they have not had sex for over six years, while Dan said he lost his sexual desire for his wife years ago, though he could not recall the exact moment. Dan wanted to stay married but Nancy had her doubts.

Nancy's Core Complaint: *He seems uninterested in me. Most of the time, he keeps his distance. He does not pay attention to me and we don't often connect. He consistently seems to be more involved in the kids than with me.*

Dan's Core Complaint: *She never seems to be happy with me. She says I'm to blame for everything. I can't offer her all she wants.*

Core Descriptors: What adjectives would you use to describe your parents?

Nancy unwittingly described her mother the same way she described her husband. The unfinished business she had with her mother was redirected to Dan. It is also important to note that all of the women in Nancy's family had never been happy with their men. It seemed like Nancy carried over this pattern to her marriage.

Nancy's Core Descriptors: *She was emotionally distant and I never felt that we bonded. I cannot approach her when I need something. She does not know how to take care of me.*

On the other hand, Dan had merged with his mother because of the absence of his father. Dan became the man he thought his mother needed, even when he was still a young boy. He also pushed his father away because of this which resulted in him pushing away his foundation of masculinity.

Dan's Core Descriptors: *My mother was too needy. She always wanted more from me. Meanwhile, my father was weak. He cannot level with the men in my mom's family.*

Core Sentence: What is your greatest fear? What do you think is the worst thing that could happen to you?

Nancy's Core Sentence: *I fear that I would get stuck in a sad marriage and feel alone.*

Nancy's fear stems back to her grandmother who had been miserable in her marriage with Nancy's alcoholic grandfather. Her grandpa was blamed for every wrong thing that happened in their family. She unconsciously carried this over just as her mother carried it over with Nancy's father. But this time, Nancy chose to stop the cycle and be open to healing.

Dan's Core Sentence: *I am scared that Nancy might leave me or that she would die. I do not want to live without her.*

Meanwhile, Dan's core sentence originated from his mother's fear of being left alone at ten years old when his grandmother died. In some way, this pattern repeated when Dan's mother was hospitalized for six weeks as Dan turned ten. He carried this fear throughout adulthood and into their marriage.

<u>Core Trauma</u>: What tragedies happened in your family history?

It is a must that we see the family system to identify the core trauma. Nancy is the third generation in her family to be simply dissatisfied with their spouses. Her grandfather was dubbed as a good-for-nothing alcoholic and his father was known to be never good enough. Nancy also felt that her mother didn't give her enough, as she was more focused on taking care of Nancy's grandmother.

Dan's grandmother died when his mother was only ten. It was the reason why his mother became needy and it seemed like his father was not strong enough to provide for her mother's needs. Dan, in return, had to step up and provide what he could to his mother. He felt like his mother and his wife, Nancy, needed too much from him.

The blame-tossing started to dissipate after they realized they had brought unresolved business into their marriage. Once-leveled charges and projections were now being recognized from a wider perspective of their family's history. The delusion that the other was accountable for his or her dissatisfaction started to fade as the bigger picture became clearer to both. They have rekindled their feelings and started to show compassion toward each other.

To extend the benefits of these realizations, Dan and Nancy also made peace with their parents in each one's chosen way. Nancy used the ritual of putting her mother's photograph beside the bed to imagine being cradled by her, which is what Nancy needed when she was still a child. Dan, on the other hand, imagined being able to talk to her late mother. He imagined his mother acknowledging that she, indeed, asked beyond what he was capable of giving. These rituals and visualizations are vital to their journey toward healing.

Poet Rilke once said, "The hardest task we have to do is to love another human being. It is the final task, the ultimate test and confirmation, and the one for which all the other duties are but preparation." Our relations are likely to suffer as long as we are entangled in the web of familial habits. However, we may uncover our influences from our family history when we learn to disentangle the unseen threads that run through it, which becomes feasible by deciphering our primary language. We become more able to offer and accept love when we make what has previously been unseen visible.

Below is a list of twenty-one dynamics that affect intimacy with our partner.

Difficult relationship with mother.

It's possible that what's unresolved with your mother will happen again with your partner.

Rejected, judged, or blamed a parent.

It's possible that you subconsciously retain the behaviors, feelings, and qualities that you find unacceptable in your parents. You could blame your partner for your grievances against that parent. You can also find yourself attracted to a spouse who exhibits traits resembling the parent you were rejected by. You could struggle in your relationships to make up for your parent's rejection.

Merged with a parent's feelings.

You'll probably harbor unfavorable thoughts about your spouse if one parent has bad feelings toward the other. Dissatisfaction with a relationship can be passed down through generations.

Interrupted early bond with mother.

When you try to form an intimate connection with a spouse in this dynamic, you likely feel some level of fear. As the relationship progresses, the anxiousness frequently grows. Unaware that the anxiousness is caused by a rupture in the initial link, you may start to criticize your spouse or start other fights to get away from the intimacy.

Responsible for parents' emotions.

The child's experience of having his needs fulfilled in such a dynamic may become incidental, and the experience of being able to access his inner sentiments may be swamped by the habitual tendency to provide care rather than receive it. Later in age, this youngster can end up giving his partner too much and causing relationship stress. The inverse may also be true.

Unhappy parents.

Likely, you will not let yourself get more than your parents did if they had trouble getting along or had a difficult time as a couple. Even though you realize that what your parents want for you is pleasure, an unconscious allegiance to them may prevent you from ever being happier than they were. Children who experience minimal excitement in the home may experience shame or discomfort.

Separated parents.

You could unintentionally end your relationship if your parents didn't remain together. This can happen once you hit the same age they did when they divorced or when you've been together for the same length of time, or when your kid becomes the same age as you did when your parents divorced. Otherwise, you might live together physically but emotionally apart.

A Parent/Grandparent rejected a former partner.

If your grandfather or father abandoned a former partner or wife who was made to believe that the romance would result in a marriage, you, as the descendant, may make amends for this by also ending up alone like the jilted woman. Assuming the lady felt as if she was not good enough for Grandpa or Dad, you might also feel the same way.

Mother got brokenhearted by her great love.

You could unintentionally share your mother's grief. You can have experienced the loss of your first love, harbor your mother's lovelessness, or feel unworthy or flawed (as she did). You could believe that the companion you seek can never be yours. As the son, you could vigorously strive to take the position of the first love and act as your mother's companion.

Father got brokenhearted by his great love.

You could unintentionally share your father's pain. Additionally, you can lose your greatest love, harbor your father's love-sickness in you, or feel unworthy or flawed (as he did). You could believe that the companion you seek can never be yours. You can vigorously attempt to take the position of the first love and turn into a companion to your father as the daughter.

A Parent/Grandparent stayed alone.

You could choose to live alone if one of your grandparents or parents did after being abandoned or following the passing of their spouse. You could cause tension or distance in a relationship if you want to feel alone. You instinctively discover a method to absorb the loneliness in quiet loyalty.

Parent/Grandparent suffered in marriage.

For instance, your grandfather may have been an alcoholic, passed away, engaged in gambling, or abandoned your grandmother, leaving her in a loveless marriage. You could automatically equate these events with marriage if your grandma raised her children by herself. You could either go through what she did or decide not to commit to a partner out of concern that it might happen to you.

Parent disrespected by another parent.

You may relive your parent's experience if you are disrespected by your spouse.

The parent died early.

When you attain the same age as the deceased parent, when you've been in a relationship for the same length of time, or when your kid reaches the same age as you were when your parent died, you could emotionally or physically separate yourself from your spouse.

One parent mistreated the other.

To convince yourself that your father isn't "the evil one" alone, you, the son, can treat your spouse badly if your father mistreats your mother. You can have a spouse that treats you badly or whom you don't feel connected to as the daughter. It could be challenging for you to be happier than your mother.

You hurt a past partner.

If you badly hurt a former lover, you could unintentionally try to make up for it by ruining your current relationship.

You had too many partners.

If you've been with too many people, your capacity to connect in a relationship may have been damaged. Separations may get simpler. Relationships can become shallow.

Had an abortion or gave away a child for adoption.

You could not let yourself have much joy in a relationship because of your shame, regret, or remorse.

Becoming mother's confidante.

When you were a young boy, you made an effort to meet your mother's unmet needs and give her what she thought she couldn't obtain from your father. Later, you could find it challenging to commit to a lady. You can withdraw emotionally or physically out of concern that your spouse will demand too much of you as your mother did.

Father's favorite.

A girl who has a stronger bond with her father than she does her mother frequently feels unsatisfied with the men she chooses. The estrangement she suffers from her mother is the real issue—not the boyfriend. The quality of a woman's bond with her mom can predict how rewarding her relationship with her spouse will be.

Someone in the family ended up alone.

You could be connected to a grandparent, aunt, uncle, older sibling, or parent who never wed. It's possible that this individual was derided, made fun of, or thought to be inferior to the other members of the family. Inadvertently aligned, you could also avoid getting married.

Lessons

1. Our romantic relationships can be affected by our family's past.

2. We are bound to recreate our parents' and grandparents' problems with our present relationships.

3. It is important to acknowledge that our relationship is different from our grandparents' and parents' relationships. Their pain belongs to them and it shouldn't have the capacity to affect us

Issues Surrounding the Subject Matter

1. Why is it important to pinpoint the similarities of our relationship to the relationship of your parents (and grandparents, if applicable)?

2. What is your biggest complaint about your partner? Why do you think of him that way?

3. What adjectives would you use to describe your partner? Would you use the same words to describe one of your parents?

Goals

1. How do your relationship problems reflect the problems of your parents before?

2. What would your spouse's core language map look like?

3. How would you feel once you have made the connection between your relationship problems to your past?

Action Steps

1. <u>Analyze if your relationship mirrors the same pattern as your family history.</u> If you are having relationship troubles, it could be related to your family's past. Ask the following questions:

   - Listen to the words you use when you complain about your partner (without judgment). Do the words sound familiar?
   - Do you use the same words to describe your mother or father?

- Do your grandparents and/or parents use the same complaints about one another?
- Do you see a parallel pattern between the three generations?
- Does your experience mirror the experience you had as a child (with your parents)?

2. Create a core language map for your spouse. It should look as follows:

- *Spouse's Core Complaint:*
- *Spouse's Core Descriptors:*
- *Spouse's Core Sentence*
- *Spouse's Bridging Questions:*
- *Spouse's Core Trauma*

3. Create a genogram for you and your spouse, both paternal and maternal sides. Compare the results. Discuss the similarities you will observe. Ask yourselves what needs to change.

Checklist

1. Just like you did, tell your spouse to prepare a pen and notebook for him/her so you could work together on resolving your issues.

2. Together with your partner, research and learn about your family histories. It will help you understand the issues that you both brought into the relationship.

3. Be open-minded and listen to each other's concerns. Communication is key.

Ch 13: The Core Language of Success

Summary

Most self-help books promise ultimate success if only we would follow the author's step-by-step plan. But what about us who never seem to succeed regardless of how hard we try to follow the rules? Research shows us that, most of the time, the reason behind failure might be that we identified with someone who constantly failed, was cheated on, or cheated on someone else.

It is important to differentiate your core language from your fear of success and failure. It will help you to get back on your feet just like Ben. Ben is a lawyer who was behind in paying his bills and barely surviving. His core language was: *I am just merely surviving. I barely have enough*. His core language brought him back to his grandfather who lived in Florida.

His grandfather started a plantation that made him a rich man. But while his grandfather lived in the big mansion, his workers were not compensated for their hard work. Ben even remembered playing with the workers' kids while carrying the guilt. Eventually, his grandfather died and his father inherited the estate. But due to failed business decisions, his father lost everything, which meant Ben did not inherit anything.

When he made the connection, Wolynn asked Ben to visualize the kids he used to play with, their parents, and his grandfather in one picture. He imagined his grandfather apologizing to the families and even to Ben himself. As he let go of this burden, which was not even his in the first place, he donated to a charity for migrant families. He also took a pro-bono case to help someone who has been exploited by a large corporation.

Following that event, big clients started to reach out to him. Within six months, his career flourished. For Ben, his core language brought him back to his grandfather's hometown. Unfortunately, not everyone who wants to go further can find a family event that is so explicitly marked, just like John-Paul.

Although skilled and talented, John-Paul was never noticed by the upper management of his company. This was because JP did his best to play safe and stay under the radar. His core language was: *If I make the wrong move, I might be rejected and would lose everything.* Going back to his childhood, it turned out that JP and his mother were separated for a brief moment.

His parents went on a vacation and left little JP under the care of his grandparents. Although his grandparents provided him with everything he needed, they rarely ever spent time with him. They went on to do their chores, etc. To make matters worse, JP's grandfather suddenly got sick, which further divided his grandmother's attention. When his parents arrived, he was already detached and conscious of every move he made.

Having gotten used to not being a bother or concern to anyone else in his life, he learned to walk on eggshells around people. This behavior stayed with him until he started working. The betrayal and failure he felt when he was left alone forced him to put up walls around himself. He thought that it would protect him from getting hurt and disappointed. When he made this link, JP had to heal the inner image he carried of her mother. He recalled how delighted his mom would be when he drew her pictures.

Our connection with success can be impacted by a variety of factors, including rifts in our mother-child relationship, as John-Paul experienced as well as unethical business practices and unfair inheritances, as Ben did. But these are only some examples of how family ties affect our success.

Here are other dynamics that could negatively impact our success:

Rejecting a parent.

Whatever the cause, when we reject our parents, we also reduce the chances available to us of succeeding in relationships, at work, or at enjoying life. We may unintentionally alienate ourselves from life's pleasures when we shun our mother. A son who has rejected his father may have anxiety or self-consciousness around other males as a result. Work and social lives can both be hampered by unresolved issues with our parents. Unconsciously reliving unresolved family dynamics increases the likelihood of conflict rather than forging genuine bonds.

Repeating a rejected parent's life experience.

Once we reject a parent, we may unintentionally walk in their shoes. We believe that the contrary is true: the further we are from our parents, the less probable it is that we will follow in their footsteps and face the same difficulties. The opposite, though, seems to be more accurate. We tend to resemble them more and live lifestyles that are like theirs when we separate ourselves from them.

Being unconsciously loyal to failure.

Rejection is not necessary to repeat the same mistakes as our parents. We occasionally have an unspoken connection that keeps us stuck in a similar situation. We could discover that, despite our greatest efforts, we are unable to surpass what they were able to do in their life. Imagine if your father is unsuccessful and is unable to provide for the rest of your family. You could sabotage your success with the fear of surpassing your father because of this loyalty to failure.

Continuing the legacy of unfinished business.

If someone in the family dies unexpectedly early and is believed to not have succeeded in living his life completely, there is a chance that someone in later generations might also fail something big in life. The latter family member may give up before completing a life goal, such as earning a degree or closing a contract that would lead to success.

Past poverty dimming present success.

Sometimes we unconsciously align ourselves with ancestors who struggled to support themselves and their offspring while living in poverty. If our ancestors experienced immense sorrow, we may unknowingly perpetuate their misery, and our efforts to live full lives may be frustrated. It might be challenging to own more than they did.

Suppressing success due to personal guilt.

Sometimes we have directly exploited someone or harmed them in such a way that caused them great sorrow. It's possible that we obtained an unjustified sum of money via deceit or trickery. We frequently find ourselves unable to hold onto this cash benefit when such a thing occurs. We and our children or even just our children might choose to live modest lives to make up for the harm we've caused, whether we are guilty or not or whether we think about the effects of our actions or not.

To conclude, all of the dynamics mentioned above could greatly impact our path toward success, which is why healing is important. Once we connect our present with the past, we must take the necessary step to resolve the issue within us. We need to accept that this trauma belongs to the past and that we are destined for more.

Lessons

1. No matter how hard we try, we tend to fail at succeeding in life mainly because we have some unfinished business with our parents or we do not want to achieve more than they did.

2. Sometimes, it's fear that holds us back from success.

3. We need to accept that our parents' hardships do not belong to us.

Issues Surrounding the Subject Matter

1. Does your status in life parallel what your parents experienced when you were a child?

2. Why are you self-sabotaging your success?

3. What are the financial issues that your family and other ancestors faced before?

Goals

1. How does your past affect your achievements and dreams?

2. How are you going to work hard to achieve the success that your parents did not?

3. How are you going to accept that you are not responsible for your parents' failures?

Action Steps

1. Revisit your core descriptors in Chapter 7. Answer the following questions:

   - Did you have a difficult relationship with your mother?
   - Did you have a difficult relationship with your father?

2. With the questions above, determine which of the mentioned dynamics you can relate to the most.

3. Make peace with your parents' (and grandparents') failures. You may use the healing sentences and rituals in the previous chapters.

Checklist

1. Research the twenty success questions from the book *It Didn't Start With You*. Use them as a guide to identifying your family dynamics.

2. If your ancestors have ever hurt or gained wealth at the expense of a minority group, you may want to research a charity that supports the minority and give them assistance (in any way).

3. Honor the struggles of your ancestors, regardless of whether you are fully aware of them or not. Acknowledging and honoring them would be enough.

Ch 14: Core Language Medicine

Summary

This book offers a fresh approach to listening that sheds light on the gloomy passageways of the past. We can determine what relates to us and what could have originated from a traumatic incident in our family background by learning how to interpret our core language map. Old patterns may be let go once their source is known, allowing new paths to a new and better life to emerge.

You may now revisit the worries you previously jotted down in the hopes that you feel better or more at peace today than you ever did. With family members you've met along the way, you could feel more sympathy or a feeling of belonging. They could be supporting you differently today. Perhaps you can sense their warmth and support. Spend a moment feeling this comfort. Send your breath to the parts of your body that are experiencing it. You are currently home to these new emotions, and they need your attention and care to grow.

You can keep untangling from the chain of inherited anxiety once your core phrase and its origin are in conscious awareness. What formerly served as an unconscious chant keeping you imprisoned in sorrow can now serve as a tool to release you. Simply put the following advice into practice if you start to sense the old emotions coming back.

It is also encouraged for you to go back to the previous chapters that particularly struck you. For the new ideas, pictures, and sensations to stick with you and stabilize you through the highs and lows of daily life, you must revisit the rituals and resolve sentences to further anchor and deepen the healing.

You could be standing on the opposite side of your darkest fear if you followed the advice in this book. This can resemble being on a mountain peak and looking down into a valley. The area may be seen in its entirety from the distance, as though through a wide-angle lens. The past anxieties, the present panic, the tragedies and heartbreaks of the family are down in the valley. All of the pieces of the family history may be viewed and accepted from this fresh perspective.

You've probably found major connections by piecing together key pieces of knowledge about your family. You now know more about who you are and the irrational sensations you've experienced. In all likelihood, they didn't begin with you. Perhaps you've also come to realize that, after listening to its instructions, your darkest fear is no longer so terrifying.

Now that you realize it, you can stop using your covert language of fear. The greater mystery is that a tremendous love was there all along, ready to be unearthed. It is the love that those who lived before you handed on to you, a love that demands that you enjoy your life to the fullest without experiencing the same anxieties and tragedies as in the past. It is a profound affection. It is a gentle love that lasts forever and binds you to everyone and everything.

Lessons

1. Your trauma is not yours. It may have come from the previous generation's unresolved trauma.

2. It is up to you to stop the cycle of pain. It is up to you to make the change.

3. Acknowledgment and comprehension are enough to move on.

Issues Surrounding the Subject Matter

1. Why is it important to recognize the images, thoughts, and sensations from within?

2. What are your next steps? How will you maintain the peace?

3. What is the most impactful lesson you have gained?

Goals

1. How are you going to recognize the images, thoughts, and sensations from within?

2. How are you going to acknowledge that the fear you have isn't yours? Rather, it is only activated because of a trigger.

3. How are you going to disentangle from a spiraling emotion?

Action Steps

1. Review what you've written in the core language map. Acknowledge that everything you ever felt is not yours.

2. Extend your compassion to the affected family members. They may be at fault for not resolving matters on their own, but understand that it was also difficult for them. Comprehend that, like you, they might also be victims of a recurring pattern.

3. Forgive yourself. You have spent the past chapters accepting people who have brought you pain. It is only fair that you also accept and forgive yourself for the negative thoughts you have. Write down everything you want to say to yourself.

Checklist

1. Keep the notes in your notebook. If ever you're having a hard time again, it's easier for you to repeat the same steps you took.

2. Continue the healing rituals you have set up. Go beyond healing. Learn to live happily and without heavy thoughts.

3. Spread the word to those people whom you think need it, too. People with insomnia, depression, suicidal thoughts, etc

Epilogue

It is human nature to push away those who have brought us pain, regardless if we are biologically related to them or not. We immediately assume that the best way to heal is through distance and isolation. *It Didn't Start With You* proves that this notion couldn't be further from the truth.

It turns out that our trauma may not even be ours in the first place. When a tragedy happens in our family and those immediately affected fail to resolve it in their time, it tends to be inherited by the following generations. It is not fair to us but that's how epigenetics and cellular biology work. This has been proven by various case studies presented in the workbook, including the children and grandchildren of parents who suffered from PTSD.

The results of the research mentioned in this workbook also highlight the importance of building a healthy and stable parent-child relationship, from the womb up to the early childhood years. Those formative years are vital to the overall emotional, physical, and psychological health of the children. As parents, it is your prime responsibility to ensure that your offspring are well-nurtured, secured, and most importantly, loved.

We have read the stories of depressed and suicidal individuals who have been carrying the guilt, trauma, and sins of their grandparents, parents, aunts, uncles, and other members of their family system. The narratives show us that the first step we need to make is to acknowledge that the pain we are feeling does not belong to us. It belongs to the previous generations and is something that needed to stay with them.

This workbook teaches us that the most effective key to self-healing is acceptance and making peace. Distancing ourselves and pushing our family away does not help us break the cycle of family trauma. Mark Wolynn, the author himself, shared how he made a conscious effort to rebuild the relationship he had with his estranged parents. He found peace and so did many others.

It Didn't Start With You does not promise success or ultimate happiness. But it gives us the means to achieve what we all crave – peace of mind. And based on real-life examples, once you've set self-healing into motion, everything else follows. The trauma may not have begun with us but ending it is up to us.

Made in the USA
Las Vegas, NV
10 August 2023

75915415R00083